B-1B La

"The Bone"

Detailed instructions on how to build the B-1B Lancer 1/48 scale from Revell. This book also includes instructions for adding Eduard's BIG ED PE Set, Eduard Brassin Sniper ATP, along with the following kits from Barracuda; Late Exhaust Set, Engine Intake Set, External Upgrade Set, and the Main & Nose Wheel Set. In addition to the mask set in the BIG ED, I also have masks from New Ware and Furball. THIS BOOK CAN BE ALSO BE USED FOR MODEL 5714

Special Thanks to the B-1B Builder's Support Group

I highly recommend joining the B-1B Builder's Support Group on Facebook. As of this printing, they had almost 900 members who have built or are currently building this kit. There are B-1B experts who can provide details of the actual aircraft. The modelers also suggest paint and marking variations of the various B-1B squadrons and the aircraft versions. They post lots of photos and point out any issues with their build including aftermarket kits. They maintain a complete list of aftermarket kits for the B-1B model. If you are interested in some really cool modifications, check out how some members added lights, flaps, and escape hatches. Feel free to ask questions. The members are very helpful. So if you have this kit (and this book) - join this Facebook group right away.

Contents

B-1B Lancer History

The Rockwell B-1 Lancer is a supersonic variable-sweep wing, heavy bomber used by the United States Air Force. It is commonly called the "Bone" (from "B-One"). It is one of three strategic bombers in the U.S. Air Force fleet as of 2018, the other two being the B-2 Spirit and the B-52 Stratofortress.

The B-1 was first envisioned in the 1960s as a platform that would combine the Mach 2 speed of the B-58 Hustler with the range and payload of the B-52, and would ultimately replace both bombers. After a long series of studies, Rockwell International (now part of Boeing) won the design contest for what emerged as the B-1A. This version had a top speed of Mach 2.2 at high altitude and the capability of flying for long distances at Mach 0.85 at very low altitudes. The combination of the high cost of the aircraft, the introduction of the AGM-86 cruise missile that flew the same basic profile, and early work on the stealth bomber all significantly affected the need for the B-1. This led to the program being canceled in 1977, after the B-1A prototypes had been built.

The program was restarted in 1981, largely as an interim measure until the stealth bomber entered service. This led to a redesign as the B-1B, which had lower top speed at high altitude of Mach 1.25, but improved low-altitude performance of Mach 0.96. The electronics were also extensively improved during the redesign, and the airframe was improved to allow takeoff with the maximum possible fuel and weapons load. The B-1B began deliveries in 1986 and formally entered service with Strategic Air Command (SAC) as a nuclear bomber in 1986. By 1988, all 100 aircraft had been delivered.

In the early 1990s, following the Gulf War and concurrent with the disestablishment of SAC and its reassignment to the newly formed Air Combat Command, the B-1B was converted to conventional bombing use. It first served in combat during Operation Desert Fox in 1998 and again during the NATO action in Kosovo the following year. The B-1B has supported U.S. and NATO military forces in Afghanistan and Iraq. The Air Force had 66 B-1Bs in service as of September 2012. The B-1B is expected to continue to serve into the 2030s, with the Northrop Grumman B-21 Raider to begin replacing the B-1B after 2025. The B-1s currently in inventory will be retired by 2036.

Variants

B-1A

The B-1A was the original B-1 design with variable engine intakes and Mach 2.2 top speed. Four prototypes were built; no production units were manufactured.

B-1B

The B-1B is a revised B-1 design with reduced radar signature and a top speed of Mach 1.25. It is optimized for low-level penetration. A total of 100 B-1Bs were produced.

B-1R

The B-1R was a proposed upgrade of existing B-1B aircraft. The B-1R (R for "regional") would be fitted with advanced radars, air-to-air missiles, and new Pratt & Whitney F119 engines. This variant would have a top speed of Mach 2.2, but with 20% shorter range. Existing external hardpoints would be modified to allow multiple conventional weapons to be carried, increasing overall loadout. For air-to-air defense, an active electronically scanned array (AESA) radar would be added and some existing hardpoints modified to carry air-to-air missiles. If needed the B-1R could escape from unfavorable air-to-air encounters with its Mach 2+ speed. Few aircraft are capable of sustained speeds over Mach 2. **From Wikipedia**

By United States Air Force photo by Staff Sgt. Bennie J. Davis III

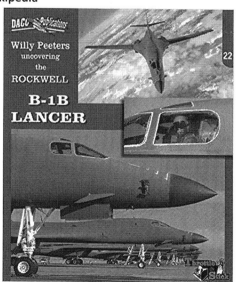

Get this great reference book

Model Kit Contents

There are 4 large sprues that Revell has cut up to fit in plastic bags. There is a sprue containing the clear canopy pieces and a fifth sprue with the tires. In addition to the kit parts, I'm including the following after-market parts.

Eduard Photo Etch

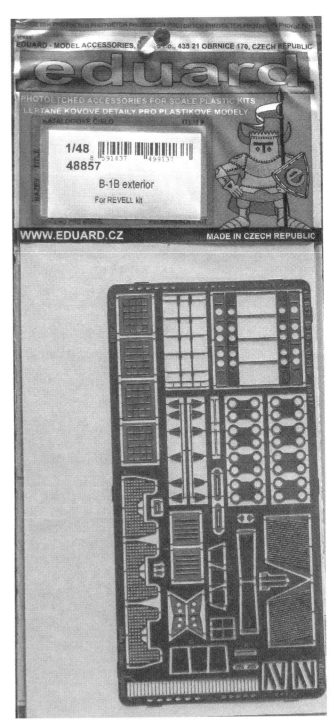

Barracuda

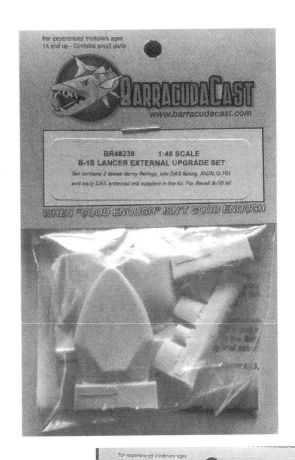

Eduard Brassin

SHAPEWAYS

Shapeways Pylon

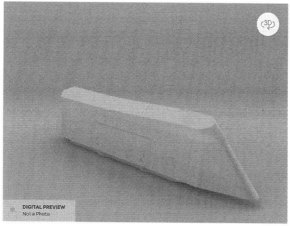

1:48 Scale Pylon for B-1B Sniper Pod

Made by
BaconFistModels

$7.00

Smooth Fine Detail Plastic ▼

3D printed in matte translucent plastic that showcases fine and intricate details.

QTY 1 ▼   BUY NOW

Smooth Fine Detail Plastic

7

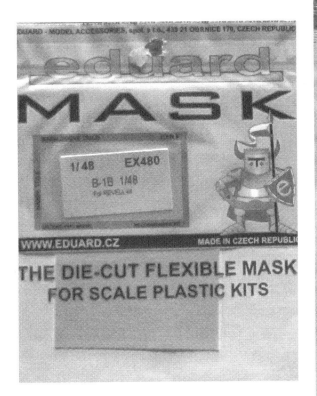

This is the decal sheet supplied with the model

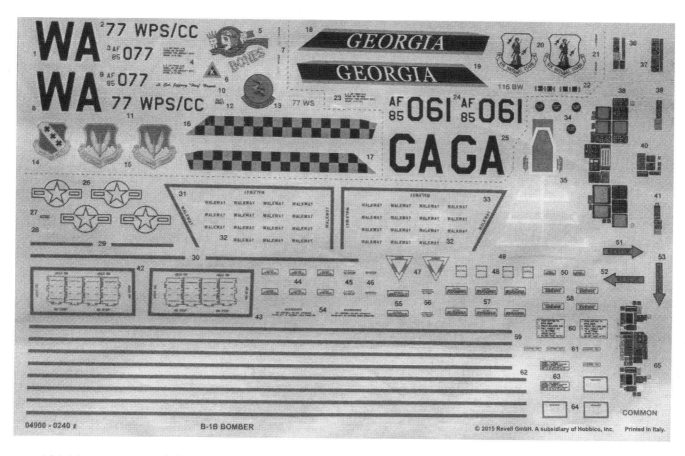

I highly recommend that you scan the decal sheets into your computer as a high resolution image. Hopefully, the decal application step will go smooth but just in case there's an issue and you need another decal, you can print the image on some decal paper.

Get Organized

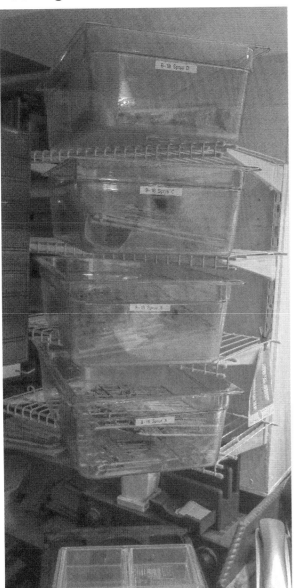

After inspecting the box contents and add-on kits, I like to break them out and place them into individual tote trays. I don't have to worry about working from the box or having them sprawled across my workstation and possibly getting damaged. Depending of the size of the sprue sheets, I have different sets of tote trays. For the larger sprues (like this B-1B model), I have some clear cold food pans that are 21 x 13 inches arranged on some wire shelves. For smaller sprues and some aftermarket parts, I have a nice rolling tray cart that is normally used by beauty salons that is perfect for plastic modeling. I also have some small kitty litter pans that are great for staging partially assembled parts. I put the photo etch frets in a set of clear jewelry drawers.

Rolling cart containing 5 tote trays with the different sprue sheets. A great way to stay organized and protect the parts from damage. I label each tray and also attach a label to each sprue. I use this for most of my builds

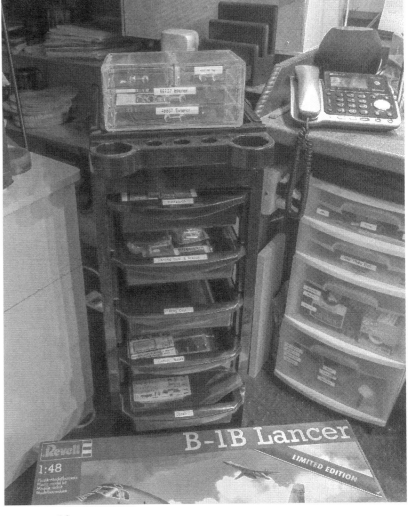

Model Build

Build Flow

This model is huge. It is much bigger than most workbenches. The fuselage is 36 inches long and with the wings fully extended, the width is 35 inches. So we're going to break the build into 3 major sections - Wings, Fuselage, and Engines

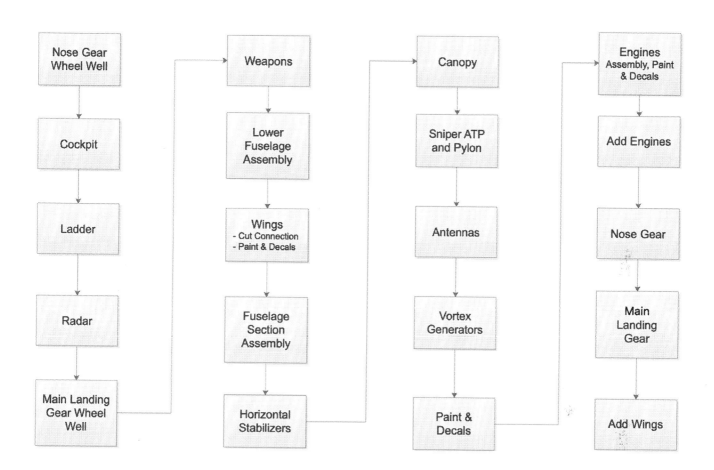

Paints

No.	Paint Color	My Substitute Recommendation (Most are Tamiya unless specified)	Your Paint
	Gray Primer	Surface Primer (Light Gray)	
	White Primer	Surface Primer (White)	
	Clear Coat	TS-13 Clear or X-22 Clear	
	Flat Coat	TS-80 Flat Clear	
	Semi-gloss Coat	TS-79 Semi-gloss Clear	
	Silver Weathering	Tamiya Weathering Master 87085	
	Soot Weathering	Tamiya Weathering Master 87080	
	Exhaust Wash	AK Exhaust Wash	
	Cold Gray Wash	MIG Cold Grey Wash	
	Clear Red	X-27 Clear red	
	Clear Green	X-25 Clear Green	
	Gun Metal	X-10 Gun Metal	
	Burnt Jet Engine Pigment	AK Burnt Jet Engine Pigment	
A	Anthracite Grey, Matt (Revell 9)	XF-69 or TS-63 Nato Black	
B	Light Grey, Matt (Revell 76)	XF-75 IJN Gray or TS-66 IJN Gray	
C*	Anthracite Grey, Matt (Revell 9) (25%) and Steel Metallic (Revell 91) (75%)	TS-42 Light Gun Metal	
D*	Gunship Gray, Matt (Revell 74) (75%) Clear Gloss (Revell 1) (25%)	TS-99 IJN Gray or XF-87 IJN Gray	
E	Mouse Grey, Matt (Revell 47)	XF-77 IJN Gray or TS-67 IJN Gray	
F	White, Silky-Matt (Revell 301)	X-2 White or TS-26 Pure White	
G	Carmine Red, Matt (Revell 36)	XF-7 Flat Red or TS-85 Bright Red	
H	Yellow, Matt (Revell 15)	XF-3 Flat Yellow or TS-34 Camel Yellow	
I	Fiery red, Silky-Matt (Revell 330)	X-7 Red or TS-8 Italian Red	
J	Leaf Green, Silky-Matt (Revell 364)	XF-67 NATO Green or AS-23 Light Green	
K	Gold Metallic (Revell 94)	X-12 Gold Leaf or TS-21 Gold	
L	Aluminum Metallic (Revell 99)	XF-16 Flat Aluminum or TS-30 Silver Leaf	
M	Steel Metallic (Revell 91)	X-11 Chrome Silver or TS-83 Metallic Silver	
N *	Green, Silky-Matt (Revell 360) (75%) and Bronze Green, Matt (Revell 65) (25%)	XF-67 NATO Green or AS-23 Light Green Luftwaffe	
O*	Dark Grey, Silky-Matt (Revell 378) (80%) and Black, Silky-Matt (Revell 302) (20%)	XF-85 Rubber Black or TS-82 Black Rubber	
P	Silver Metallic (Revell 90)	X-11 Chrome Silver or TS-83 Metallic Silver	
Q	Beige, Silky-Matt (Revell 314)	XF-78 Wooden Deck - TS-68 Wooden Deck Tan	

*Using the iModelKit App on an iPAD, I found the hex code for each color. Using the online color mixing tool (trycolors.com), I plugged in the two hex codes and the percentages to get the new color. I compared the new color to a sample of all of the Tamiya spray paints and selected the closest match.

Tools

Here is a typical list of tools I used to build most models and where I bought them

Name	Tool Type	Possible Source (Where I purchased)
Tamiya Sharp Pointed Side Cutter 74035	Cutters	Amazon
God Hand Ultimate Nipper 5.0 Plastic model Tools for GH-SPN-120	Cutter	Amazon
Tamiya 74052 Decal Tweezers	Tweezers	Amazon
Tamiya 74048 HG Straight Tweezers	Tweezers	Amazon
Tamiya 74047 HG Angled Tweezers	Tweezers	Amazon
Tamiya 74102 HG Angled Tweezers Reverse Action w/ grooved mouth	Tweezers	Amazon
Pearl Tweezer Item #: 82426	Tweezers	Micro-Mark
Hold & Place Pencil	Holding Tools	ParaGrafix.
Pic-N-Stic	Holding Tools	Pulpdent
Gripster Nut Starter Item #: 21116A	Holding Tools	Micro-Mark
Holding Tool for Micro Size Parts Item #:80770	Holding Tools	Micro-Mark
Magiclasp Forceps Item #:82488	Holding Tools	Micro-Mark
X-ACTO Designer Series #1 Hobby and Craft Knife (X3254)	Knives, Scalpels, & Razors	Amazon
Techni Edge #11 Hobby Blades- 100 Pack	Knives, Scalpels, & Razors	Amazon
S-1310, 10cm Round Premium Stainless Steel Surgical Scalpel Handles	Knives, Scalpels, & Razors	Havel
S-1330, 10cm Hexagonal Premium Stainless Steel Surgical Handles	Knives, Scalpels, & Razors	Havel
SC6100, Sterile Carbon Steel Miniature Surgical Blades - 100 Blades	Knives, Scalpels, & Razors	Havel
SC6700, Sterile Carbon Steel Miniature Surgical Blades - 100 Blades	Knives, Scalpels, & Razors	Havel
SC6200, Sterile Carbon Steel Miniature Surgical Blades - 100 Blades	Knives, Scalpels, & Razors	Havel
SC6700MIS Sterile Carbon Steel Miniature Surgical Blades - 100 Blades	Knives, Scalpels, & Razors	Havel
Tamiya 74031 Decal Scissors 4-1/2 inches	Scissors	Amazon
Squizzers Item # 81204	Scissors	Micro-Mark
SCR01 Scriber	Panel Scribers	UMM-USA
SCR02 Scriber	Panel Scribers	UMM-USA
SCR03 Scriber	Panel Scribers	UMM-USA
General's Ultra Tech Precision Power Screwdriver Item #: 86258	Drills	Micro-Mark
Drill Chuck for Ultra Tech Precision Power Screwdriver Item #: 86259	Drills	Micro-Mark
Rogers which has 20 bits (#61 thru #80). Item # 82416	Drills	Micro-Mark
HTS (Model 104S1) Clamp	Clamps	Amazon
Coffee Stirrers	Paint Shakers/Stirrers	Amazon
Electric Paint Shaker, 110-Volt AC Powered by Robart	Paint Shakers/Stirrers	Amazon
Badger Air-Brush Co. 121 Paint Mixer	Paint Shakers/Stirrers	Amazon
Tamiya #87071 size No.1	Paint Brushes	HobbyInc
Tamiya #87072 size No. 0	Paint Brushes	HobbyInc
Tamiya #87073 size No. 00	Paint Brushes	HobbyInc
Tamiya #87074 size No. 000	Paint Brushes	HobbyInc
Da Vinci Series 5361 Russian Red Sable Miniature Detail Paint Brush Set with sizes 10/0, 5/0, 4/0, 3/0, and 2/0.	Paint Brushes	Amazon
La Corneille Miniature Micro Detail Brush 5 Pc Set By Loew Cornell	Paint Brushes	Amazon

Name	Tool Type	Possible Source (Where I purchased)
Plaid One Stroke Brush Set, Pack of 10 (Donna Dewberry)	Paint Brushes	Amazon
Loew-Cornell Soft Comfort Brush 18/0 Taklon Spotter (6-Pack)	Paint Brushes	Amazon
Parts and Brush Washer Item #:85152	Paint Brush Cleaners	Micro-Mark
Masters Brush Cleaner	Paint Brush Cleaners	Amazon
Micro Brush Regular Size Green Product No. MHR10	Micro Brushes	HobbyInc
Micro Brush Fine Size Yellow Product No. MHF10	Micro Brushes	Amazon
Micro Brush Superfine Size White Product No. MHS10	Micro Brushes	HobbyInc
Ultra Brush applicators (Black Product No. MHU10)	Micro Brushes	HobbyInc
Glass Eyedroppers	Eyedroppers	Amazon
Model-Expo (MET1017) Dust Brush	Dust Brushes	HobbyInc
Tamiya (TAM74078) Dust Brush	Dust Brushes	Amazon
PanaVise Model 201 "Junior" Miniature Vise	Assembly Stands	Amazon
PanaVise 312 Tray Base Mount	Assembly Stands	Amazon
PanaVise 204 Neoprene Pads	Assembly Stands	Amazon
PanaVise 239 Speed Control Handle	Assembly Stands	Amazon
PanaVise 300 Standard Bases	Assembly Stands	Amazon
PanaVise 305 Low Profile Base	Assembly Stands	Amazon
PanaVise 337 Fixturing Head.	Assembly Stands	Amazon
JH4801 for 1/32 and 1/48 scale aircraft	Assembly Stands	UMM-USA
VMP002 Plastic stand and transport jig for 1/32 scale aircraft	Assembly Stands	UMM-USA
Triple Duty Foam Cradle for Model Ships Item #: 85819	Assembly Stands	Micro-Mark
Master Airbrush Smooth Rotating 7-1/2" Diameter Revolving Turntable	Painting Stands	Amazon
MR. ALMIGHTY CLIPS II stand	Painting Stands	Amazon
Blu-Tack	Blu-Tack	Amazon
SMS004 Photo Etch Bending Tool 5.5" (5 Speed) Hold and Fold with 16 Bending Finger Options	Photo-Etch	Small Shop
SMS002 Photo Etch Bending Tool The "BUG" RTH Hold and Fold that has 2" X 2 ½" Base with a Full 2" Square Tool Head	Photo-Etch	Small Shop
SMS006 Photo Etch Bending & Rolling Deluxe Brass Assist for shaping radius, U-Shape or cylinder parts.	Photo-Etch	Small Shop
5 in razor blade	Photo-Etch	Small Shop
SMS015 Photo Etch Cut-Off Set	Photo-Etch	Small Shop
SMS016 Photo Etch Cut-Off Set	Photo-Etch	Small Shop
Tamiya Mini Bending Pliers for PE Part TAM74084	Photo-Etch	Amazon
Tamiya 74066 Diamond File For Photo Etched Parts	Photo-Etch	Amazon
Tamiya 74068 PE scissors	Photo-Etch	Amazon
.2 mm black Micron 005 pen	Panel Markers	Amazon
Kneading Eraser	Kneading Eraser	Amazon
Silly Putty	Silly Putty	Amazon
Tamiya Extra Thin Cement	Glue	Amazon
Microscale's Micro Liquitape	Glue	Bare Metal

Name	Tool Type	Possible Source (Where I purchased)
VMS Flexy 5K CA Photo Etch CA Cement	Glue	Michigan Toy Soldier
VMS Flexy 5K CA Diorama CA Cement	Glue	Michigan Toy Soldier
VMS Flexy 5K CA Resin CA Cement	Glue	Michigan Toy Soldier
VMS Styrene Cement Standard	Glue	Michigan Toy Soldier
Micro Set	Decal Solutions	Bare Metal
Micro Sol	Decal Solutions	Bare Metal
Mr Mark Setter	Decal Solutions	Ebay
Mr Mark Softer	Decal Solutions	Ebay
6 mm- TAM87030	Masking Tape	HobbyInc
10 mm- TAM87031	Masking Tape	HobbyInc
18 mm- TAM87032	Masking Tape	HobbyInc
40 mm- TAM87063	Masking Tape	HobbyInc
Mr Masking Sol Neo	Liquid Mask	Ebay
Micro Mask	Liquid Mask	Bare Metal
Fasmask	Liquid Mask	AAA Hobbies
Lead Wire - Round Various thicknesses	Lead Wire	UMM-USA
Lead Wire - Flat Various thicknesses	Lead Wire	UMM-USA
Deluxe Perfect Plastic Putty	Putty	Amazon
Sanding Sticks	Sanding	HobbyInc
Sanding Needles	Sanding	AAA Hobbies
Sanding Twigs Item 84425	Sanding	Micro-Mark
Flex-I-File	Sanding	Flex-I-File
2 inch square foam pads	Sanding	HobbyInc
3M 9211	Dust Mask	Amazon
Rust Oleum Lacquer Thinner	Lacquer Thinner	Home Depot
Raven Nitrile gloves	Gloves	Amazon
Cotton Gloves	Gloves	Amazon
Q-Tips	Q-Tips	Supermarket
Alcohol	Alcohol	Supermarket
Toothpicks	Toothpicks	Supermarket
Small Plastic Plates	Small Plastic Plates	Sam's Club
Styrene - Various	Styrene	HobbyInc
Artograph 1530 Hobby Model Spray Booth	Paint Spray Booth	Engineering Supply
ROLL FILTER TRAY 30"	Paint Spray Booth	Micro-Mark
Iwata HP-TH	Airbrush Equipment	Amazon
Silent Aire DR150 air compressor	Airbrush Equipment	Art Supply Source
Weller TB100 Soldering Gun	Photo Etch	Micro-Mark
Tix Flux & Solder	Photo Etch	Micro Mark
Larger Bending Mandrel Set	Photo Etch	Micro Mark

Sequential Steps

Follow these steps in order to build your perfect model. Good luck. There are 778 steps in the instructions. Steps for the after market items will be colored in gray so if you don't have these after market kits, just skip the gray steps.

Please use pages 16 to 157 to make a mark in the Done column indicating that you completed that step.

Step	Instruction	Source	Done
1.	Assuming you have the sprues separated and organized, I recommend putting them into a tote tray (small kitty litter pan or dish pan will work too). Fill the tray with cool water and some dish soap. Let them soak for 30 minutes or so. Rinse them off with cool water and set aside on a drying mat or towel overnight until they are completely dry.	M&P	
		Figure 1	
2.	Ultimately, we're going to finish with configuration A	O	
M&P = Marking and Painting, O = Optional, Aftermarket in Gray			

Step	Instruction	Source	Done
		Figure 2	
3.	Paint A5, A6, and A7 with white primer	M&P	
4.	Paint A5, A6, and A7 with TS-26 Pure White	M&P	
5.	Using photos of an actual Bone, paint the raised surfaces and apply weathering. I recommend using the photos in Willy Peeters uncovering the Rockwell B-1B Lancer	O, M&P	
6.	Dry fit A7 to A6 as shown in "Figure 2" on page 17	Section 2	
7.	Glue A7 to A6 as shown in "Figure 2" on page 17	Section 2	
8.	Dry fit A5 to A6 as shown in "Figure 2" on page 17	Section 2	
9.	Glue A5 to A6 as shown in "Figure 2" on page 17. In future steps, this will be referred to as Assembly 2.	Section 2	
M&P = Marking and Painting, O = Optional, Aftermarket in Gray			

Step	Instruction	Source	Done

Figure 3

Step	Instruction	Source	Done
10.	Paint A8, A9, and A10 with white primer	M&P	
11.	Paint A8, A9, and A10 with TS-26 Pure White	M&P	
12.	Using photos of an actual Bone, paint the raised surfaces and apply weathering. I recommend using the photos in Willy Peeters uncovering the Rockwell B-1B Lancer	O, M&P	
13.	Dry fit A10 to Assembly 2 as shown in "Figure 3" on page 18	Section 3	
14.	Glue A10 to Assembly 2 as shown in "Figure 3" on page 18	Section 3	
15.	Dry fit A9 to A10 (do not glue) as shown in "Figure 3" on page 18	Section 3	
16.	Dry fit A8 to Assembly 2 and A9 as shown in "Figure 3" on page 18	Section 3	
17.	Glue A8 to Assembly 2 as shown in "Figure 3" on page 18.In future steps, this will be referred to as Assembly 3.	Section 3	
M&P = Marking and Painting, O = Optional, Aftermarket in Gray			

Step	Instruction	Source	Done

Figure 4

Step	Instruction	Source	
18.	Paint A11 and A12 with white primer	M&P	
19.	Paint A11 and A12 with TS-26 Pure White	M&P	
20.	Using photos of an actual Bone, paint the raised surfaces and apply weathering. I recommend using the photos in Willy Peeters uncovering the Rockwell B-1B Lancer	O, M&P	
21.	Dry fit A11 to Assembly 3 as shown in "Figure 4" on page 19	Section 4	
22.	Glue A11 to Assembly 3 as shown in "Figure 4" on page 19	Section 4	
23.	Dry fit A12 to Assembly 3 as shown in "Figure 4" on page 19	Section 4	
24.	Glue A12 to Assembly 3 as shown in "Figure 4" on page 19. In future steps, this will be referred to as Assembly 4.	Section 4	
M&P = Marking and Painting, O = Optional, Aftermarket in Gray			

Step	Instruction	Source	Done

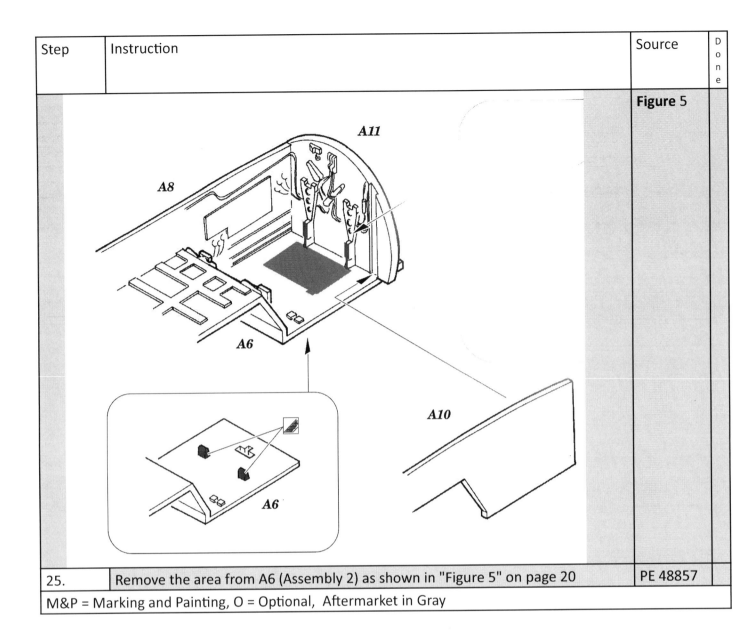

Figure 5

Step	Instruction	Source	Done
25.	Remove the area from A6 (Assembly 2) as shown in "Figure 5" on page 20	PE 48857	

M&P = Marking and Painting, O = Optional, Aftermarket in Gray

Step	Instruction	Source	Done
		Figure 6	

26.	Dry fit 33 to A6 as shown in "Figure 6" on page 21	PE 48857	
27.	Glue 33 to A6 as shown in "Figure 6" on page 21	PE 48857	
28.	Form and dry fit 29 (2pcs) to A11 as shown in "Figure 6" on page 21. I had a hard time getting 29 to bridge the gap between 33 and sit flush on A11. I had to break it in two. I glued the back piece to A11. I glued the bottom of the front piece to 33, leaned it back to A11, and glued it to the back piece on A11	PE 48857	
29.	Glue 29 (2pcs) to A11 as shown in "Figure 6" on page 21	PE 48857	
M&P = Marking and Painting, O = Optional, Aftermarket in Gray			

Step	Instruction	Source	D o n e
		Figure 7	
30.	First measure 44mm from the inside edge of A11 down each side of A8 and A10 and make a mark. Cut a slot about 4mm long thru the raised areas in the sides of A8 and A10 as shown in "Figure 7" on page 22. You can also double check the position by dry fitting the nose gear wheel well up against B28	PE 48857	
31.	Form and dry fit 22 to the slot in A8 as shown in "Figure 7" on page 22	PE 48857	
32.	Glue 22 to the slot in A8 as shown in "Figure 7" on page 22	PE 48857	
M&P = Marking and Painting, O = Optional, Aftermarket in Gray			

Step	Instruction	Source	Done
33.	Form and dry fit 22 to the slot in A10 as shown in "Figure 7" on page 22	PE 48857	
34.	Glue 22 to the slot in A10 as shown in "Figure 7" on page 22	PE 48857	
		Figure 8	
35.	Form and dry fit 43 to A12 (Assembly 4) as shown in "Figure 8" on page 23	PE 48857	
36.	Glue 43 to A12 (Assembly 3) as shown in "Figure 8" on page 23	PE 48857	
37.	Paint the PE added to Assembly 4 with X-2 White	M&P	
M&P = Marking and Painting, O = Optional, Aftermarket in Gray			

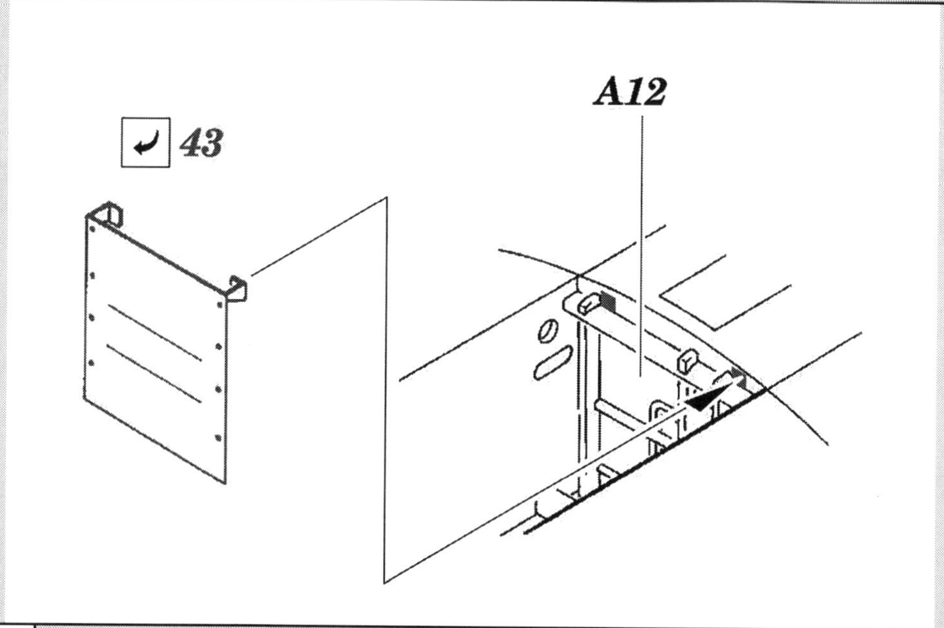

Step	Instruction	Source	Done

You need to protect the hinges for the nose gear wheel well door (see circles) from damage while adding future components. I recommend jamming a piece of foam rubber in the opening so it sticks out past the hinges.

M&P = Marking and Painting, O = Optional, Aftermarket in Gray

Step	Instruction	Source	Done
		Figure 9	

38.	Make 4 seat assemblies - Dry fit B13 to B14 as shown in "Figure 9" on page 25	Section 5	
39.	Dry fit B15 to B13 as shown in "Figure 9" on page 25	Section 5	
40.	Glue B15, B13, and B14 as shown in "Figure 9" on page 25. These seat assemblies will be referred to as Assembly 5 in future steps.	Section 5	
41.	Paint each seat assembly with gray primer	M&P	
42.	Paint each seat assembly with TS-66 IJN Gray	M&P	
43.	Paint the area of B15 with XF-69 NATO Black as shown in "Figure 9" on page 25	M&P	
44.	Paint the area of B15 with XF-3 Flat Yellow as shown in "Figure 9" on page 25 **(Skip if you have PE)**	M&P	
45.	Paint the area of B14 with XF-3 Flat Yellow as shown in "Figure 9" on page 25 **(Skip if you have PE)**	M&P	
46.	Paint the area of B14 with X-7 Red as shown in "Figure 9" on page 25	M&P	
47.	Paint the area of B13 with XF-7 Flat Red as shown in "Figure 9" on page 25	M&P	
48.	Paint the area of B13 with XF-67 NATO Green as shown in "Figure 9" on page 25. **(Skip if you have PE)**	M&P	
M&P = Marking and Painting, O = Optional, Aftermarket in Gray			

Step	Instruction	Source	Done

Figure 10

B13, B14, B15

Step	Instruction	Source	Done
49.	Grind down the areas on each seat as shown in "Figure 10" on page 26	PE 49737	
50.	Form and dry fit 4 on the top left of each seat as shown in "Figure 10" on page 26	PE 49737	
51.	Glue 4 on the top left of each seat as shown in "Figure 10" on page 26	PE 49737	
52.	Form and dry fit 4 on the top right of each seat as shown in "Figure 10" on page 26	PE 49737	
53.	Glue 4 on the top right of each seat as shown in "Figure 10" on page 26	PE 49737	
54.	Form and dry fit 10 to each seat as shown in "Figure 10" on page 26	PE 49737	
55.	Glue 10 to each seat as shown in "Figure 10" on page 26	PE 49737	
M&P = Marking and Painting, O = Optional, Aftermarket in Gray			

Step	Instruction	Source	Done

Figure 11

B13, B14,
B15

Step	Instruction	Source	Done
56.	Form and dry fit 14 on the left side of the seat cushion on each seat assembly as shown in "Figure 11" on page 27	PE 49737	
57.	Glue 14 on the left side of the seat cushion on each seat assembly as shown in "Figure 11" on page 27	PE 49737	
58.	Form and dry fit 14 on the right side of the seat cushion on each seat assembly as shown in "Figure 11" on page 27	PE 49737	
59.	Glue 14 on the right side of the seat cushion on each seat assembly as shown in "Figure 11" on page 27	PE 49737	
60.	Form and dry fit 17 on the left side of the seat cushion on each seat assembly as shown in "Figure 11" on page 27	PE 49737	
61.	Glue 17 on the left side of the seat cushion on each seat assembly as shown in "Figure 11" on page 27	PE 49737	
62.	Form and dry fit 15 on the right side of the seat cushion on each seat assembly as shown in "Figure 11" on page 27	PE 49737	
63.	Glue 15 on the right side of the seat cushion on each seat assembly as shown in "Figure 11" on page 27	PE 49737	
M&P = Marking and Painting, O = Optional, Aftermarket in Gray			

Step	Instruction	Source	Done
		Figure 12	

16

2

18

13

13

B13, B14, B15

Step	Instruction	Source	Done
64.	Form and dry fit 2 to the right side of each seat assembly as shown in "Figure 12" on page 28	PE 49737	
65.	Glue 2 to the right side of each seat assembly as shown in "Figure 12" on page 28	PE 49737	
66.	Form and dry fit 13 to the right side of each seat assembly as shown in "Figure 12" on page 28	PE 49737	
67.	Glue 13 to the right side of each seat assembly as shown in "Figure 12" on page 28	PE 49737	
68.	Form and dry fit 13 to the left side of each seat assembly as shown in "Figure 12" on page 28	PE 49737	
69.	Glue 13 to the left side of each seat assembly as shown in "Figure 12" on page 28	PE 49737	
70.	Form and dry fit 16 to the right side of each seat assembly as shown in "Figure 12" on page 28	PE 49737	
71.	Glue 16 to the right side of each seat assembly as shown in "Figure 12" on page 28	PE 49737	
72.	Form and dry fit 18 to the left side of each seat assembly as shown in "Figure 12" on page 28	PE 49737	

M&P = Marking and Painting, O = Optional, Aftermarket in Gray

Step	Instruction	Source	Done
73.	Glue 18 to the left side of each seat assembly as shown in "Figure 12" on page 28	PE 49737	
		Figure 13	
74.	Paint B17, B19, and B18 with gray primer (skip B18 if you have PE)	M&P	
75.	Paint B17 with TS-82 Black Rubber	M&P	
76.	Paint areas of B17 with XF-75 IJN Gray as shown in "Figure 13" on page 29 **(Skip if you have PE)**	M&P	
77.	Paint B17 with TS-13 Clear **(Skip if you have PE)**	M&P	
78.	Apply the following decals to B17: 39, 40, & 41 as shown in "Figure 13" on page 29 **(Skip if you have PE)**	M&P	
79.	Paint B17 with TS-80 Flat Clear **(Skip if you have PE)**	M&P	
80.	Paint B19 with TS-63 NATO Black	M&P	
81.	Paint B18 with TS-66 IJN Gray **(Skip if you have PE)**	M&P	
82.	Paint controls on B18 with XF-69 NATO Black as shown in "Figure 13" on page 29 **(Skip if you have PE)**	M&P	
83.	Paint B18 with TS-13 Clear **(Skip if you have PE)**	M&P	
84.	Apply decal 65 to B18 as shown in "Figure 13" on page 29 **(Skip if you have PE)**	M&P	
85.	Paint B18 with TS-80 Flat Clear **(Skip if you have PE)**	M&P	
M&P = Marking and Painting, O = Optional, Aftermarket in Gray			

Step	Instruction	Source	Done
86.	Grind down the raised controls on B17 and B18 as shown in "Figure 14" on page 30 and as shown in "Figure 15" on page 31	PE 49737	
87.	Dry fit B18 to B19 as shown in "Figure 13" on page 29	Section 6	
88.	Glue B18 to B19 as shown in "Figure 13" on page 29	Section 6	
89.	Dry fit B18/B19 to B17 as shown in "Figure 13" on page 29 (Remove if you have PE)	Section 6	
90.	Glue B18/B19 to B17 as shown in "Figure 13" on page 29 **(Skip if you have PE)**	Section 6	
91.	Paint B16 (2 pcs) with XF-69 NATO Black	M&P	
92.	Paint the top of B16 with X-7 Red as shown in "Figure 13" on page 29	M&P	
93.	Dry fit B16 to the left side of B17 as shown in "Figure 13" on page 29	Section 6	
94.	Glue B16 to the left side of B17 as shown in "Figure 13" on page 29	Section 6	
95.	Dry fit B16 to the right side of B17 as shown in "Figure 13" on page 29	Section 6	
96.	Glue B16 to the right side of B17 as shown in "Figure 13" on page 29. This assembly will be referred to as Assembly 6 in future steps.	Section 6	
		Figure 14	

B18

19

1

B17

19

M&P = Marking and Painting, O = Optional, Aftermarket in Gray

Step	Instruction	Source	Done
97.	Note: parts 1 thru 13 on 49737 are self adhesive. So when I say to glue these parts, I mean to press them firmly into place which activates the glue. However, I recommend applying a drop of CA anyway.	PE 49737	
98.	Form 19 (4 pcs) as shown in "Figure 14" on page 30	PE 49737	
99.	Dry fit 19 (2 pcs) to the left side of B17 as shown in "Figure 14" on page 30	PE 49737	
100.	Glue 19 (2 pcs) to the left side of B17 as shown in "Figure 14" on page 30	PE 49737	
101.	Dry fit 19 (2 pcs) to the right side of B17 as shown in "Figure 14" on page 30	PE 49737	
102.	Glue 19 (2 pcs) to the right side of B17 as shown in "Figure 14" on page 30	PE 49737	
103.	Dry fit 1 to B18 as shown in "Figure 14" on page 30	PE 49737	
104.	Glue B18/B19 to B17 as shown in "Figure 13" on page 29	PE 49737	
		Figure 15	
105.	Dry fit 6 to B17 as shown in "Figure 15" on page 31	PE 49737	
106.	Glue 6 to B17 as shown in "Figure 15" on page 31	PE 49737	
107.	Dry fit 12 to B17 as shown in "Figure 15" on page 31	PE 49737	
108.	Glue 12 to B17 as shown in "Figure 15" on page 31	PE 49737	
109.	Dry fit 11 to B17 as shown in "Figure 15" on page 31	PE 49737	
110.	Glue 11 to B17 as shown in "Figure 15" on page 31	PE 49737	

M&P = Marking and Painting, O = Optional, Aftermarket in Gray

Step	Instruction	Source	D o n e
		Figure 16	
111.	If you consider yourself as a Photo Etch Expert, then follow the steps below as outlined by Eduard. If not, form each 7 to a box, break each 3 into two pieces, form each 3 and glue them separately in each 7 (two per).	O	
112.	Form 7 (2 pcs) as shown in "Figure 16" on page 32	PE 49737	
113.	Form 3 (4 pcs) and dry fit into 7 (2 per) as shown in "Figure 16" on page 32	PE 49737	
114.	Glue 3 to 7 (2 per) as shown in "Figure 16" on page 32	PE 49737	
115.	Dry fit 7 to 11 as shown in "Figure 16" on page 32	PE 49737	
116.	Glue 7 to 11 as shown in "Figure 16" on page 32	PE 49737	
117.	Dry fit 7 to 6 as shown in "Figure 16" on page 32	PE 49737	
118.	Glue 7 to 6 as shown in "Figure 16" on page 32	PE 49737	
M&P = Marking and Painting, O = Optional, Aftermarket in Gray			

Step	Instruction	Source	Done
7		**Figure** 17	

119.	Paint B20 with gray primer	M&P	
120.	Paint B20 with TS-82 Black Rubber	M&P	
121.	Dry fit 2 Assembly 5 seats to Assembly 6 as shown in "Figure 17" on page 33	Section 7	
122.	Glue 2 Assembly 5 seats to Assembly 6 as shown in "Figure 17" on page 33	Section 7	
123.	Dry fit B20 to Assembly 6 as shown in "Figure 17" on page 33	Section 7	
124.	Glue B20 to Assembly 6 as shown in "Figure 17" on page 33. This assembly will be referred to as Assembly 7 in future steps.	Section 7	
M&P = Marking and Painting, O = Optional, Aftermarket in Gray			

Step	Instruction	Source	Done
		Figure 18	

125.	Paint B21, B22, and B23 with gray primer	M&P	
126.	Paint B21 with TS-66 IJN Gray	M&P	
127.	Paint the controls on B21 with XF-69 NATO Black as shown in "Figure 18" on page 34 **(skip if you have PE)**	M&P	
128.	Paint B21 with TS-13 Clear **(skip if you have PE)**	M&P	
129.	Apply decal 38 to B21 **(skip if you have PE)**	M&P	
130.	Paint B21 with TS-80 Flat Clear **(skip if you have PE)**	M&P	
131.	Paint B22 and B23 with TS-82 Black Rubber	M&P	
132.	Paint the control areas of B22 and B23 with XF75 IJN Gray as shown in "Figure 18" on page 34	M&P	
133.	Paint B22 and B23 with TS-13 Clear **(skip if you have PE)**	M&P	
134.	Apply decal 36 to B22 as shown in "Figure 18" on page 34 **(skip if you have PE)**	M&P	
135.	Apply decal 37 to B23 as shown in "Figure 18" on page 34 **(skip if you have PE)**	M&P	
136.	Paint B22 and B23 with TS-80 Flat Clear **(skip if you have PE)**	M&P	
137.	Grind down the raised controls on B21 as shown in "Figure 19" on page 35	PE 49737	
138.	Dry fit B23 to B21 as shown in "Figure 18" on page 34	Section 8	
M&P = Marking and Painting, O = Optional, Aftermarket in Gray			

Step	Instruction	Source	Done
139.	Glue B23 to B21 as shown in "Figure 18" on page 34	Section 8	
140.	Dry fit B22 to B21 as shown in "Figure 18" on page 34	Section 8	
141.	Glue B22 to B21 as shown in "Figure 18" on page 34	Section 8	
142.	Dry fit one of the Assembly 5 seats to B23 as shown in "Figure 18" on page 34	Section 8	
143.	Glue one of the Assembly 5 seats to B23 as shown in "Figure 18" on page 34	Section 8	
144.	Dry fit one of the Assembly 5 seats to B22 as shown in "Figure 18" on page 34	Section 8	
145.	Glue one of the Assembly 5 seats to B22 as shown in "Figure 18" on page 34. This assembly will be referred to as Assembly 8 in future steps.	Section 8	

Figure 19

Step	Instruction	Source	Done
146.	Paint 20 and 21 with XF-75 IJN Gray	M&P	
147.	Dry fit 9 to B21 as shown in "Figure 19" on page 35	PE 49737	
148.	Glue 9 to B21 as shown in "Figure 19" on page 35	PE 49737	
149.	Dry fit 8 to B21 as shown in "Figure 19" on page 35	PE 49737	
150.	Glue 8 to B21 as shown in "Figure 19" on page 35	PE 49737	
151.	Dry fit 5 to B21 as shown in "Figure 19" on page 35	PE 49737	
152.	Glue 5 to B21 as shown in "Figure 19" on page 35	PE 49737	
153.	Dry fit 20 to B21 as shown in "Figure 19" on page 35	PE 49737	
154.	Glue 20 to B21 as shown in "Figure 19" on page 35	PE 49737	
155.	Dry fit 21 to B21 as shown in "Figure 19" on page 35	PE 49737	
156.	Glue 21 to B21 as shown in "Figure 19" on page 35	PE 49737	

M&P = Marking and Painting, O = Optional, Aftermarket in Gray

Step	Instruction	Source	D o n e

Figure 20

Step	Instruction	Source	Done
157.	Grind down the raised control area on B22 as shown in "Figure 20" on page 36	PE 49737	
158.	Repaint as needed	M&P	
159.	Paint 23 (2 pcs) with XF-16 Flat Aluminum	M&P	
160.	Dry fit 23 to B22 as shown in "Figure 20" on page 36	PE 49737	
161.	Glue 23 to B22 as shown in "Figure 20" on page 36	PE 49737	
162.	Grind down the raised control area on B23 as shown in "Figure 20" on page 36	PE 49737	
163.	Repaint as needed	M&P	
164.	Dry fit 23 to B23 as shown in "Figure 20" on page 36	PE 49737	
165.	Glue 23 to B23 as shown in "Figure 20" on page 36	PE 49737	

Figure 21

Step	Instruction	Source	Done
166.	Dry fit 24 to B25 as shown in "Figure 21" on page 36	PE 49737	
167.	Glue 24 to B25 as shown in "Figure 21" on page 36	PE 49737	

M&P = Marking and Painting, O = Optional, Aftermarket in Gray

Step	Instruction	Source	Done

Figure 22

168.	Paint B24 and B25 with gray primer	M&P	
169.	Paint B24 with TS-66 IJN Gray	M&P	
170.	Paint B25 with TS-83 Black Rubber	M&P	
171.	Dry fit B24 to Assembly 8 as shown in "Figure 22" on page 37	Section 9	
172.	Glue B24 to Assembly 8 as shown in "Figure 22" on page 37	Section 9	
173.	Dry fit B25 to Assembly 8 as shown in "Figure 22" on page 37	Section 9	
174.	Glue B25 to Assembly 8 as shown in "Figure 22" on page 37. This assembly will be referred to as Assembly 9 in future steps.	Section 9	

M&P = Marking and Painting, O = Optional, Aftermarket in Gray

Step	Instruction	Source	Done

Step	Instruction	Source	
175.	Dry fit Assembly 9 to Assembly 4 as shown in "Figure 23" on page 38	Section 10	
176.	Glue Assembly 9 to Assembly 4 as shown in "Figure 23" on page 38. This assembly will be referred to as Assembly 10 in future steps.	Section 10	
M&P = Marking and Painting, O = Optional, Aftermarket in Gray			

Step	Instruction	Source	D o n e
11 🖌		**Figure** 24	
177.	Dry fit Assembly 7 to Assembly 10 as shown in "Figure 24" on page 39	Section 11	
178.	Glue Assembly 7 to Assembly 10 as shown in "Figure 24" on page 39. This assembly will be referred to as Assembly 11 in future steps.	Section 11	
M&P = Marking and Painting, O = Optional, Aftermarket in Gray			

Step	Instruction	Source	Done

M&P = Marking and Painting, O = Optional, Aftermarket in Gray

Step	Instruction	Source	D o n e

M&P = Marking and Painting, O = Optional, Aftermarket in Gray

Step	Instruction	Source	Done

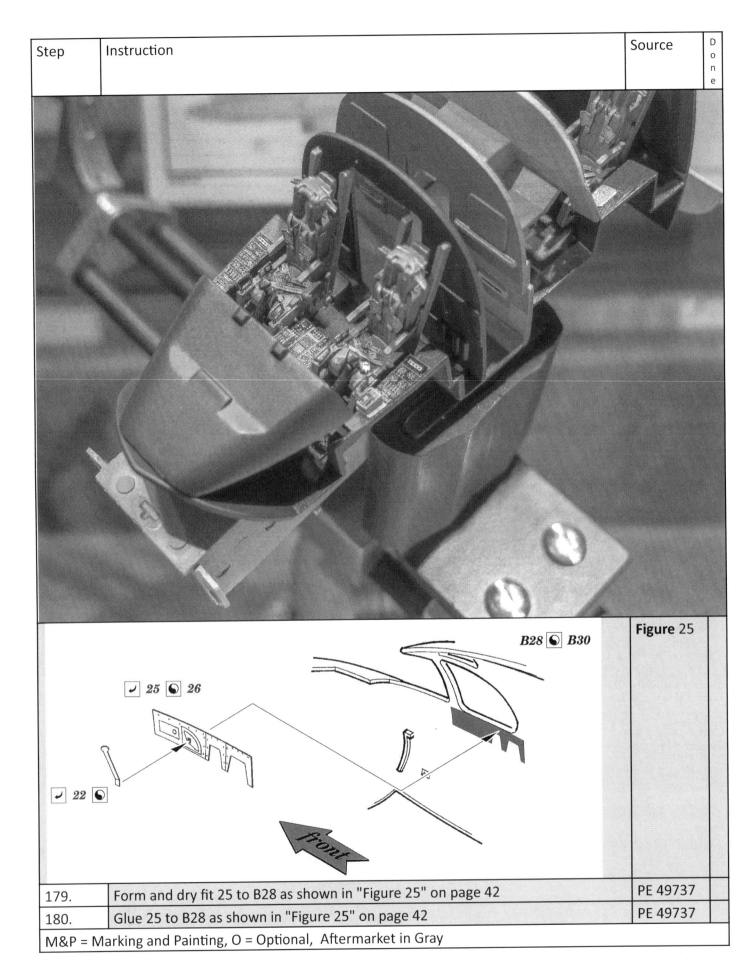

Figure 25

179.	Form and dry fit 25 to B28 as shown in "Figure 25" on page 42	PE 49737	
180.	Glue 25 to B28 as shown in "Figure 25" on page 42	PE 49737	

M&P = Marking and Painting, O = Optional, Aftermarket in Gray

Step	Instruction	Source	Done
181.	Form and dry fit 22 to 25 as shown in "Figure 25" on page 42	PE 49737	
182.	Glue 22 to 25 as shown in "Figure 25" on page 42	PE 49737	
183.	Form and dry fit 26 to B30 as shown in "Figure 25" on page 42	PE 49737	
184.	Glue 26 to B30 as shown in "Figure 25" on page 42	PE 49737	
185.	Form and dry fit 22 to 26 as shown in "Figure 25" on page 42	PE 49737	
186.	Glue 22 to 26 as shown in "Figure 25" on page 42	PE 49737	

Figure 26

Step	Instruction	Source	Done
187.	Before doing anything to B28 and B30, do a dry fit. You'll quickly discover that it is not a glove fit. I had to get one section mated, added some tape, and moved on to the next section, added some tape and so on. This will give you a plan of attack for when you add the cockpit/nose gear wheel well.	Section 16	
188.	Paint the inside of B28 with gray primer	M&P	
189.	Paint the inside of B28 with TS-66 IJN Gray	M&P	
190.	Dry fit clear part 27 to B28 as shown in "Figure 26" on page 43.	Section 12	
191.	Glue clear part 27 to B28 as shown in "Figure 26" on page 43	Section 12	
192.	Dry fit clear part 26 to B28 as shown in "Figure 26" on page 43. If you don't get a flush fit, consider cutting this piece in two and fit them separately.	Section 12	

M&P = Marking and Painting, O = Optional, Aftermarket in Gray

Step	Instruction	Source	Done
193.	Glue clear part 26 to B28 as shown in "Figure 26" on page 43. Put some masking tape on the clear parts to protect them. I used the Furball set. This assembly will be referred to as Assembly 12 in future steps.	Section 12	
	 **Figure** 27		
194.	Secure a 70g weight into Assembly 12 as shown in "Figure 27" on page 44. This assembly will be referred to as Assembly 14 in future steps.	Section 14	

For the 70g weight, I used a 2oz fishing sinker (weighed 60g on my digital scale) wrapped in some Air-Dry Clay from Crayola. This gave me 75g. I got some black Gorilla Tape and taped it to B28. Make sure it's secure...You don't want it flopping around as you work on the rest of the model.

M&P = Marking and Painting, O = Optional, Aftermarket in Gray

Step	Instruction	Source	Done
		Figure 28	
195.	Paint B30 with gray primer	M&P	
196.	Paint the inside of B30 with TS-66 IJN Gray	M&P	
197.	Dry fit clear part 27 to B30 as shown in "Figure 28" on page 45.	Section 13	
198.	Glue clear part 27 to B30 as shown in "Figure 28" on page 45	Section 13	
199.	Dry fit clear part 29 to B30 as shown in "Figure 28" on page 45. If you don't get a flush fit, consider cutting this piece in two and fit them separately.	Section 13	
200.	Glue clear part 29 to B30 as shown in "Figure 28" on page 45. Put some masking tape on the clear parts to protect them. I used the Furball set. This assembly will be referred to as Assembly 13 in future steps.	Section 13	
M&P = Marking and Painting, O = Optional, Aftermarket in Gray			

Step	Instruction	Source	D o n e
		Figure 29	
201.	Dry fit Assembly 11 to Assembly 14 as shown in "Figure 29" on page 46. If you get the front corner of Assembly 11 tucked into the raised 90 degree corner on Assembly 14 and back end on the front side of the smalled raised area, adding B30 (Assembly 13) in the next step will be easier.	Section 15	
202.	Glue Assembly 11 to Assembly 14 as shown in "Figure 29" on page 46. This assembly will be referred to as Assembly 15 in future steps.	Section 15	
M&P = Marking and Painting, O = Optional, Aftermarket in Gray			

Step	Instruction	Source	Done
		Figure 30	
203.	Paint A1, A3, A4, and the inside of B2 with white primer	M&P	
204.	Paint A1, A3, A4, and the inside of B2 with TS-26 Pure White	M&P	
205.	Paint the sections of A1, A3, and A4 with XF-75 IJN Gray as shown in "Figure 30" on page 47	M&P	
206.	Paint the sections of A1, A3, and A4 with XF-77 IJN Gray as shown in "Figure 30" on page 47	M&P	
207.	Paint the sections of A1, A3, A4, and B2 with XF-69 NATO Black as shown in "Figure 30" on page 47	M&P	
208.	Dry fit A1 to B2 as shown in "Figure 30" on page 47 **(skip if you have PE)**	Section 1	
209.	Glue A1 to B2 as shown in "Figure 30" on page 47 **(skip if you have PE)**	Section 1	
210.	Dry fit A4 to B2 as shown in "Figure 30" on page 47 **(skip if you have PE)**	Section 1	
211.	Glue A4 to B2 as shown in "Figure 30" on page 47	Section 1	
212.	Dry fit A3 to A1 & A4 as shown in "Figure 30" on page 47 (Do not glue). This assembly will be referred to as Assembly 1 in future steps.	Section 1	
M&P = Marking and Painting, O = Optional, Aftermarket in Gray			

47

Step	Instruction	Source	D o n e
		Figure 31	
213.	Dry fit Assembly 1 to Assembly 15 in a closed position. **(Skip if you have PE)**	Section 16	
214.	Dry fit Assembly 13 to Assembly 15 and 1 as shown in "Figure 31" on page 48	Section 16	
215.	Glue Assembly 13 to Assembly 15 as shown in "Figure 31" on page 48. This assembly will be referred to as Assembly 16 in future steps.	Section 16	
M&P = Marking and Painting, O = Optional, Aftermarket in Gray			

Step	Instruction	Source	Done
		Figure 32	
216.	Remove the areas of B2 as shown in "Figure 32" on page 49	PE 48857	
217.	Paint the outside of B2 with TS-99 IJN Gray	M&P	
218.	Fill the areas of B2 as shown in "Figure 32" on page 49	PE 48857	
219.	Dry fit 18 to B2 as shown in "Figure 32" on page 49	PE 48857	
220.	Glue 18 to B2 as shown in "Figure 32" on page 49	PE 48857	
221.	Form and dry fit 1 to 18 as shown in "Figure 32" on page 49	PE 48857	
222.	Glue 1 to 18 as shown in "Figure 32" on page 49	PE 48857	
223.	Form and dry fit 20 to 18 as shown in "Figure 32" on page 49 (see option below)	PE 48857	
224.	Glue 20 to 18 as shown in "Figure 32" on page 49	PE 48857	
225.	Form & dry fit 20A to 18 as shown in "Figure 32" on page 49 (see option below)	PE 48857	
226.	Glue 20A to 18 as shown in "Figure 32" on page 49	PE 48857	
227.	Repaint the inside of B2 with white primer	M&P	
228.	Repaint the inside of B2 with TS-26 Pure White	M&P	
M&P = Marking and Painting, O = Optional, Aftermarket in Gray			

Step	Instruction	Source	D o n e

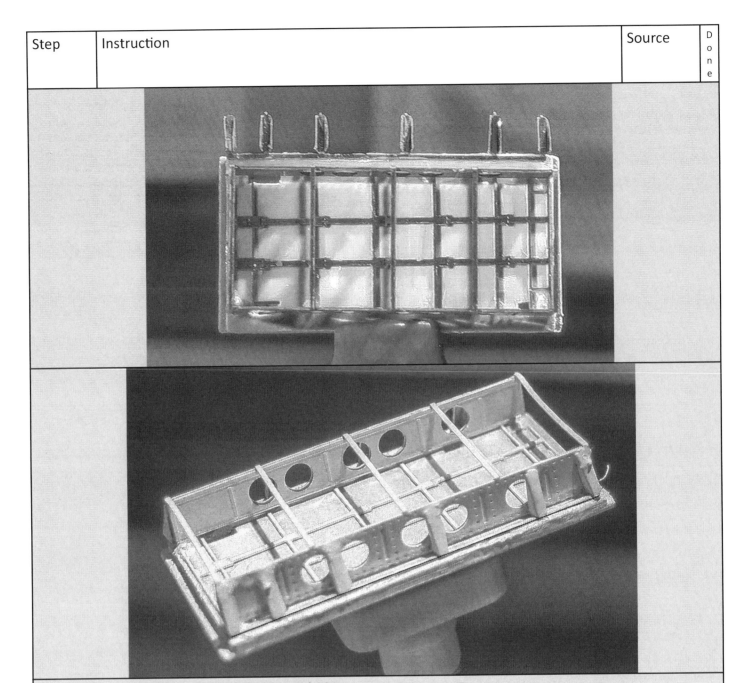

As an option, here's the way I added 20 and 20A.
- With the parts still attached to the fret, I formed the 6 support pieces. Don't fold them up on the base yet
- Cut the part from the fret
- Locate a spot halfway between 1 and the edge of B2 and lay down a narrow row of CA the length of B2 (see line in the above photo). I like to use Flexy 5K CA for Photo Etch by VMS
- Press the base of 20 (or 20a) into the CA and wait for it to harden (see the 1st photo)
- Carefully bend each of the 6 support pieces up to touch 1 and glue each piece to 1

M&P = Marking and Painting, O = Optional, Aftermarket in Gray

Step	Instruction	Source	Done
		Figure 33	

A4

A1

Consider cutting here and leaving the front intact

B2

10

A3

Step	Instruction	Source	Done
229.	Dry fit 10 to A3 as shown in "Figure 33" on page 51	PE 48857	
230.	Glue 10 to A3 as shown in "Figure 33" on page 51	PE 48857	
231.	Paint 10 with XF-69 NATO Black	PE 48857	
232.	Dry fit A3 to the B2 assembly as shown in "Figure 33" on page 51	PE 48857	
233.	Remove the sections of A4 as shown in "Figure 31" on page 48. Repaint with X-2 White as needed. Consider leaving the front part intact (see photo below)	PE 48857	
234.	Dry fit A4 to B2 assembly as shown in "Figure 33" on page 51	PE 48857	
235.	Glue A4 to B2 assembly as shown in "Figure 33" on page 51	PE 48857	
236.	Remove the sections of A1 as shown in "Figure 31" on page 48. Repaint with X-2 White as needed. Consider leaving the front part intact (see photo below)	PE 48857	
237.	Dry fit A1 to B2 assembly as shown in "Figure 33" on page 51	PE 48857	
238.	Glue A1 to B2 assembly as shown in "Figure 33" on page 51	PE 48857	
M&P = Marking and Painting, O = Optional, Aftermarket in Gray			

Step	Instruction	Source	Done
239.	This assembly will be referred to as Assembly 1 in future steps. Set this assembly aside for now. It will not fit into the fuselage in a closed position because it hits 43 (installed earlier). We'll just mask this opening when we do the major paint step.	PE 48857	

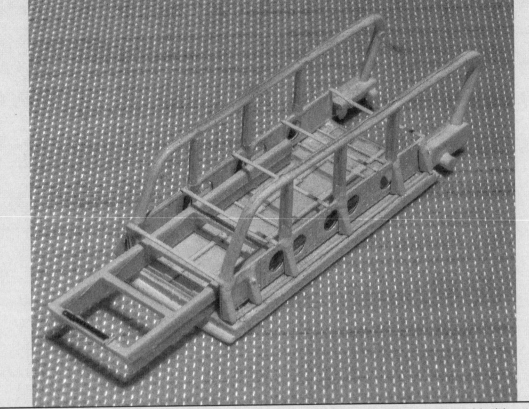

I left the top part of the railings in place and left it painted all white to match the actual ladder. I'm going to attach some flexible styrene rods to the pegs at the top so I can mount it to the opening in the fuselage.

Figure 34

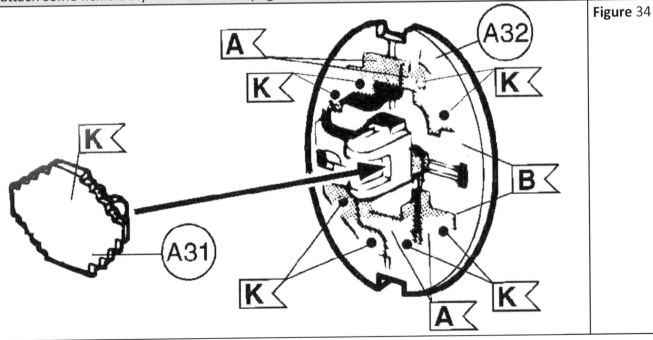

M&P = Marking and Painting, O = Optional, Aftermarket in Gray

Step	Instruction	Source	Done
240.	Paint A31 with white primer	M&P	
241.	Paint A31 with TS-21 Gold	M&P	
242.	Paint A32 with gray primer	M&P	
243.	Paint A32 with TS-66 IJN Gray	M&P	
244.	Paint areas of A32 with XF-69 NATO Black as shown in "Figure 34" on page 52	M&P	
245.	Paint areas of A32 with X-12 Gold Leaf as shown in "Figure 34" on page 52	M&P	
246.	Dry fit A31 to A32 as shown in "Figure 34" on page 52	Section 17	
247.	Glue A31 to A32 as shown in "Figure 34" on page 52. This assembly will be referred to as Assembly 17 in future steps.	Section 17	
		Figure 35	
248.	Dry fit Assembly 17 to Assembly 16 as shown in "Figure 35" on page 53	Section 18	
249.	Glue Assembly 17 to Assembly 16 as shown in "Figure 35" on page 53	Section 18	
250.	Dry fit B33 to Assembly 16 as shown in "Figure 35" on page 53. This assembly will be referred to as Assembly 18 in future steps. Note: I tried to add B33 without the radar and was alarmed about the poor fit. But after adding Assembly 17, B33 had the proper fit	Section 18	
M&P = Marking and Painting, O = Optional, Aftermarket in Gray			

Step	Instruction	Source	Done

Figure 36

A54

4 ⊙ 3

⊙ 19

⊙ 21

Step	Instruction	Source	Done
251.	Grind down the areas of A54 as shown in "Figure 36" on page 54	PE 48857	
252.	Dry fit two 19's (4 pcs) to each side of A54 as shown in "Figure 36" on page 54	PE 48857	
253.	Glue two 19's (4 pcs) to each side of A54 as shown in "Figure 36" on page 54	PE 48857	
254.	Dry fit one 21 (2 pcs) to each side of A54 as shown in "Figure 36" on page 54	PE 48857	
255.	Glue one 21 (2 pcs) to each side of A54 as shown in "Figure 36" on page 54	PE 48857	
256.	Dry fit 4 to the right side of A54 as shown in "Figure 36" on page 54	PE 48857	
257.	Glue 4 to the right side of A54 as shown in "Figure 36" on page 54	PE 48857	
258.	Dry fit 3 to the left side of A54 as shown in "Figure 36" on page 54	PE 48857	
259.	Glue 3 to the left side of A54 as shown in "Figure 36" on page 54	PE 48857	

M&P = Marking and Painting, O = Optional, Aftermarket in Gray

Step	Instruction	Source	Done

Figure 37

Step	Instruction	Source
260.	Make sure you remove the mold release circles on the front of A54 and the backs of A51 and A52	Section 29
261.	Paint A51, A52, A53, and A54 with white primer	M&P
262.	Paint A51, A52, A53, and A54 with TS-26 Pure White	M&P
263.	Paint the areas of A54 with XF-3 Flat Yellow as shown in "Figure 37" on page 55	M&P
264.	Using photos of an actual Bone, paint the raised surfaces and apply weathering. I recommend using the photos in Willy Peeters uncovering the Rockwell B-1B Lancer	O, M&P
265.	Dry fit A51 to A52 as shown in "Figure 37" on page 55	Section 29
266.	Glue A51 to A52 as shown in "Figure 37" on page 55	Section 29
267.	Dry fit A51/A52 to A54 as shown in "Figure 37" on page 55	Section 29
268.	Dry fit A53 to A54 and A51/A52 as shown in "Figure 37" on page 55	Section 29
269.	Glue A53 to A54 and A51/A52 as shown in "Figure 37" on page 55. This assembly will be referred to as Assembly 29 in future steps.	Section 29
M&P = Marking and Painting, O = Optional, Aftermarket in Gray		

Step	Instruction	Source	Done
		Figure 38	

270.	Grind down the area of A55 as shown in "Figure 38" on page 56	PE 48857	
271.	Dry fit 37 to A55 as shown in "Figure 38" on page 56	PE 48857	
272.	Glue 37 to A55 as shown in "Figure 38" on page 56	PE 48857	
273.	Grind down the area of A56 as shown in "Figure 38" on page 56	PE 48857	
274.	Dry fit 37 to A56 as shown in "Figure 38" on page 56	PE 48857	
275.	Glue 37 to A56 as shown in "Figure 38" on page 56	PE 48857	
M&P = Marking and Painting, O = Optional, Aftermarket in Gray			

Step	Instruction	Source	Done
		Figure 39	

276.	Paint A55, A56, and A57 with white primer	M&P	
277.	Paint A55, A56, and A57 with TS-26 Pure White	M&P	
278.	Paint the area of Assembly 29 XF-3 Flat Yellow as shown in "Figure 39" on page 57	M&P	
279.	Using photos of an actual Bone, paint the raised surfaces and apply weathering. I recommend using the photos in Willy Peeters uncovering the Rockwell B-1B Lancer	O, M&P	
280.	Dry fit A57 to Assembly 29 as shown in "Figure 39" on page 57	Section 30	
281.	Glue A57 to Assembly 29 as shown in "Figure 39" on page 57	Section 30	
282.	Dry fit A55 to A57 and Assembly 29 as shown in "Figure 39" on page 57	Section 30	
283.	Glue A55 to A57 and Assembly 29 as shown in "Figure 39" on page 57	Section 30	
284.	Dry fit A56 to A57 and Assembly 29 as shown in "Figure 39" on page 57	Section 30	
285.	Glue A56 to A57 and Assembly 29 as shown in "Figure 39" on page 57. This assembly will be referred to as Assembly 30 in future steps.	Section 30	
M&P = Marking and Painting, O = Optional, Aftermarket in Gray			

Step	Instruction	Source	Done

Figure 40

Step	Instruction	Source	
286.	Make 16 of the following items. Dry fit A58 to A59 as shown in "Figure 40" on page 58	Section 31	
287.	Glue A58 to A59 as shown in "Figure 40" on page 58	Section 31	
288.	Dry fit A60 to A58/A59 as shown in "Figure 40" on page 58	Section 31	
289.	Glue A60 to A58/A59 as shown in "Figure 40" on page 58. This assembly will be referred to as Assembly 31 in future steps.	Section 31	
290.	Paint the Assembly 31 pieces with white primer	M&P	
291.	Paint the Assembly 31 pieces with TS-29 Pure White	M&P	

M&P = Marking and Painting, O = Optional, Aftermarket in Gray

Step	Instruction	Source	Done
		Figure 41	
292.	Make 2 of the following assemblies. Dry fit C62 to C61 as shown in "Figure 41" on page 59	Section 32	
293.	Glue C62 to C61 as shown in "Figure 41" on page 59. This assembly will be referred to as Assembly 32 in future steps.	Section 32	
		Figure 42	
294.	Dry fit one C63 on each end of an Assembly 32 as shown in "Figure 42" on page 59	Section 33	
M&P = Marking and Painting, O = Optional, Aftermarket in Gray			

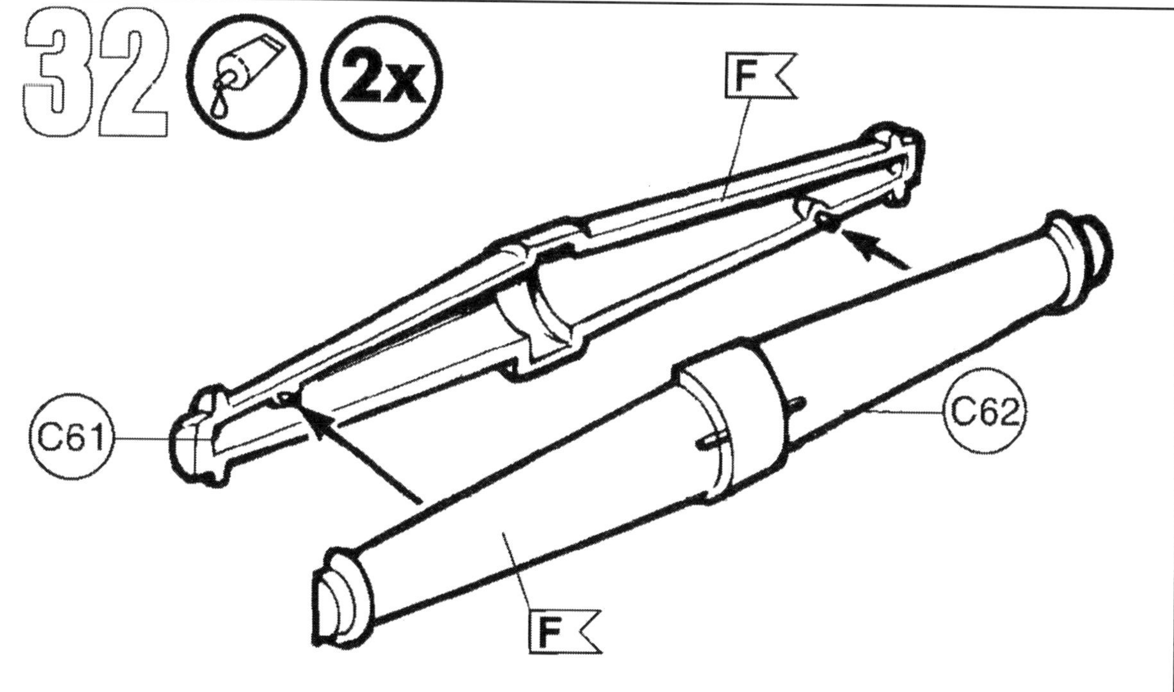

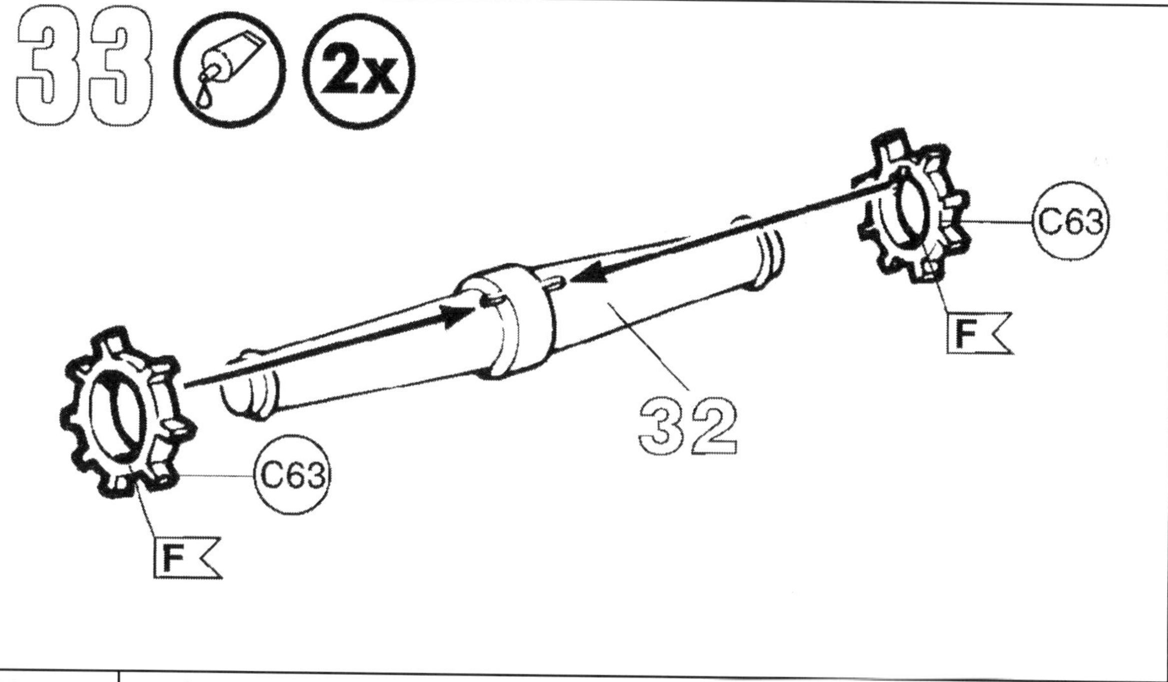

Step	Instruction	Source	Done
295.	Glue one C63 on each end of an Assembly 32 as shown in "Figure 42" on page 59. This assembly will be referred to as Assembly 33 in future steps.	Section 33	
296.	Paint each Assembly 33 with white primer	M&P	
297.	Paint each Assembly 33 with TS-26 Pure White	M&P	
		Figure 43	
298.	Make two assemblies. Dry fit 8 Assembly 31's to 1 Assembly 33 as shown in "Figure 43" on page 60	Section 34	
299.	Glue 8 Assembly 31's to 1 Assembly 33 as shown in "Figure 43" on page 60. These 2 assemblies will be referred to as Assembly 34 in future steps.	Section 34	
M&P = Marking and Painting, O = Optional, Aftermarket in Gray			

Step	Instruction	Source	D o n e
		Figure 44	

300.	Make 2 of the following assemblies. Paint A64, A65, and A66 with white primer	M&P	
301.	Paint A64, A65, and A66 with TS-26 Pure White	M&P	
302.	Paint the area of A65 and A66 with X-11 Chrome Silver as shown in "Figure 44" on page 61	M&P	
303.	Paint the area of A65 with XF-78 Wooden Deck as shown in "Figure 44" on page 61	M&P	
304.	Dry fit A65 to A66 as shown in "Figure 44" on page 61	Section 35	
305.	Glue A65 to A66 as shown in "Figure 44" on page 61	Section 35	
306.	Dry fit A64 to A66 as shown in "Figure 44" on page 61	Section 35	
307.	Glue A64 to A66 as shown in "Figure 44" on page 61. These 2 assemblies will be referred to as Assembly 35 in future steps.	Section 35	
M&P = Marking and Painting, O = Optional, Aftermarket in Gray			

Step	Instruction	Source	Done

Figure 45

Step	Instruction	Source	
308.	Make 2 sets. Dry fit 6 to A68 as shown in "Figure 45" on page 62	PE 48857	
309.	Glue 6 to A68 as shown in "Figure 45" on page 62	PE 48857	
310.	Dry fit 7 to A68 as shown in "Figure 45" on page 62	PE 48857	
311.	Glue 7 to A68 as shown in "Figure 45" on page 62	PE 48857	
312.	Dry fit 24 to A67 as shown in "Figure 45" on page 62	PE 48857	
313.	Glue 24 to A67 as shown in "Figure 45" on page 62	PE 48857	

M&P = Marking and Painting, O = Optional, Aftermarket in Gray

Step	Instruction	Source	Done
		Figure 46	
314.	Make 2 sets. Paint A67 and A68 with white primer	M&P	
315.	Paint A67 and A68 with TS-26 Pure White	M&P	
316.	Using photos of an actual Bone, paint the raised surfaces and apply weathering. I recommend using the photos in Willy Peeters uncovering the Rockwell B-1B Lancer	O, M&P	
317.	Dry fit Assembly 34 to A67 and A68 as shown in "Figure 46" on page 63	Section 36	
318.	Dry fit A67, A68 & Assembly 34 to Assembly 35 as shown in "Figure 46" on page 63	Section 36	
319.	Glue A67 to Assembly 35 as shown in "Figure 46" on page 63	Section 36	
320.	Glue Assembly 34 to A67 as shown in "Figure 46" on page 63	Section 36	
321.	Glue A68 to Assembly 35 and Assembly 34. These 2 assemblies will be referred to as Assembly 36 in future steps.	Section 36	
M&P = Marking and Painting, O = Optional, Aftermarket in Gray			

Step	Instruction	Source	Done

Figure 47

| 322. | Dry fit 2 Assembly 36's to Assembly 28 as shown in "Figure 47" on page 64 | Section 36 | |
| 323. | Glue 2 Assembly 36's to Assembly 28 as shown in "Figure 47" on page 64. I recommend adding some 2-part epoxy to the corners and ends. This Assembly will be referred to as Assembly 37 in future steps. | Section 36 | |

Figure 48

| 324. | Dry fit Assembly 30 to Assembly 37 as shown in "Figure 48" on page 64 | Section 38 | |

M&P = Marking and Painting, O = Optional, Aftermarket in Gray

Step	Instruction	Source	Done
325.	Glue Assembly 30 to Assembly 37 as shown in "Figure 48" on page 64. I recommend adding some 2-part epoxy to the corners and ends. This Assembly will be referred to as Assembly 38 in future steps.	Section 38	
		Figure 49	
326.	Dry fit C69 to C70 as shown in "Figure 49" on page 65	Section 39	
327.	Glue C69 to C70 as shown in "Figure 49" on page 65. This Assembly will be referred to as Assembly 39 in future steps.	Section 39	
328.	Paint Assembly 39 with gray primer	M&P	
329.	Paint Assembly 39 with AS-23 Light Green Luftwaffe	M&P	
M&P = Marking and Painting, O = Optional, Aftermarket in Gray			

Step	Instruction	Source	Done

Figure 50

Step	Instruction	Source	
330.	Dry fit 34 to A71 as shown in "Figure 50" on page 66	PE 48857	
331.	Glue 34 to A71 as shown in "Figure 50" on page 66	PE 48857	
332.	Dry fit 45 to A71 as shown in "Figure 50" on page 66	PE 48857	
333.	Glue 45 to A71 as shown in "Figure 50" on page 66	PE 48857	
334.	Dry fit 47 to A71 as shown in "Figure 50" on page 66	PE 48857	
335.	Glue 47 to A71 as shown in "Figure 50" on page 66	PE 48857	
336.	Dry fit 48 to A71 as shown in "Figure 50" on page 66	PE 48857	
337.	Glue 48 to A71 as shown in "Figure 50" on page 66	PE 48857	
338.	Dry fit 46 to A71 as shown in "Figure 50" on page 66	PE 48857	
339.	Glue 46 to A71 as shown in "Figure 50" on page 66	PE 48857	

M&P = Marking and Painting, O = Optional, Aftermarket in Gray

Step	Instruction	Source	D o n e
40		**Figure** 51	
340.	Paint A71 with white primer	M&P	
341.	Paint A71 with TS-26 Pure White	M&P	
342.	Using photos of an actual Bone, paint the raised surfaces and apply weathering. I recommend using the photos in Willy Peeters uncovering the Rockwell B-1B Lancer	O, M&P	
343.	Dry fit Assembly 39 to Assembly 38 as shown in "Figure 51" on page 67	Section 40	
344.	Dry fit A71 to Assembly 39 and Assembly 38 as shown in "Figure 51" on page 67	Section 40	
345.	Glue A71 to Assembly 39 and Assembly 38 as shown in "Figure 51" on page 67	Section 40	
346.	Glue Assembly 39 to Assembly 38 as shown in "Figure 51" on page 67. This Assembly will be referred to as Assembly 40 in future steps.	Section 40	
M&P = Marking and Painting, O = Optional, Aftermarket in Gray			

67

Step	Instruction	Source	Done

347.	Paint A72 (2 pcs) and A73 with white primer	M&P	
348.	Paint A72 (2 pcs) and A73 with TS-26 Pure White	M&P	
349.	Paint the area of A72 with XF-78 Wooden Deck as shown in "Figure 52" on page 68	M&P	
350.	Dry fit A72 to one side of A73 as shown in "Figure 52" on page 68	Section 41	
351.	Glue A72 to one side of A73 as shown in "Figure 52" on page 68	Section 41	
352.	Dry fit A72 to the other side of A73 as shown in "Figure 52" on page 68	Section 41	
353.	Glue A72 to the other side of A73 as shown in "Figure 52" on page 68. This Assembly will be referred to as Assembly 41 in future steps.	Section 41	
M&P = Marking and Painting, O = Optional, Aftermarket in Gray			

Step	Instruction	Source	Done

Figure 53

Step	Instruction	Source	Done
354.	Dry fit Assembly 41 to Assembly 40 as shown in "Figure 53" on page 69. Determine where and how much you need to trim as shown in "Figure 52" on page 68	Section 42	
355.	Glue Assembly 41 to Assembly 40 as shown in "Figure 53" on page 69. This Assembly will be referred to as Assembly 42 in future steps. I recommend adding some 2-part epoxy to the corners and ends.	Section 42	

M&P = Marking and Painting, O = Optional, Aftermarket in Gray

Step	Instruction	Source	Done

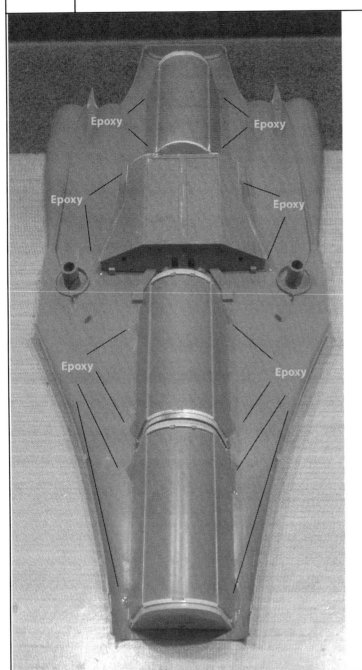

This model is big and has a lot of flex so I added some 2-part epoxy to each of the 4 major sections I also added some AK Landing Gear Wash to the main landing gear wheel well and wiped it down with AK White Spirit.

Another option to add some support is to add some styrene bracing ...see photo on the right compliments of Shawn Antunes of the B-1B Builders Support Group on Facebook.

M&P = Marking and Painting, O = Optional, Aftermarket in Gray

Step	Instruction	Source	Done
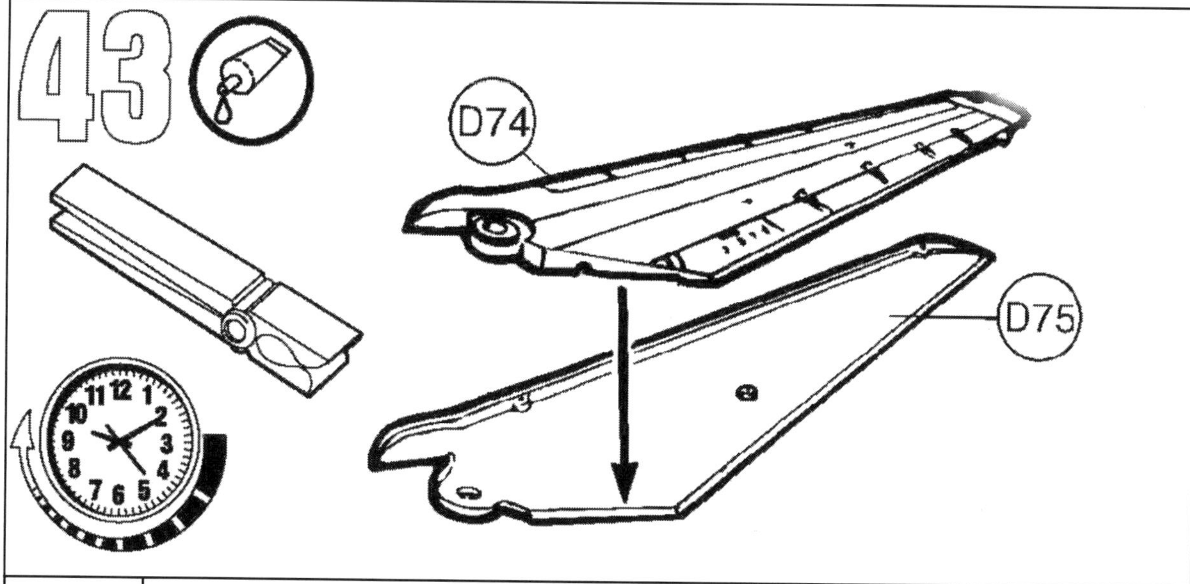 43		**Figure** 54	
356.	Dry fit D74 to D75 as shown in "Figure 54" on page 71	Section 43	
357.	Glue D74 to D75 as shown in "Figure 54" on page 71 This Assembly will be referred to as Assembly 43 in future steps.	Section 43	
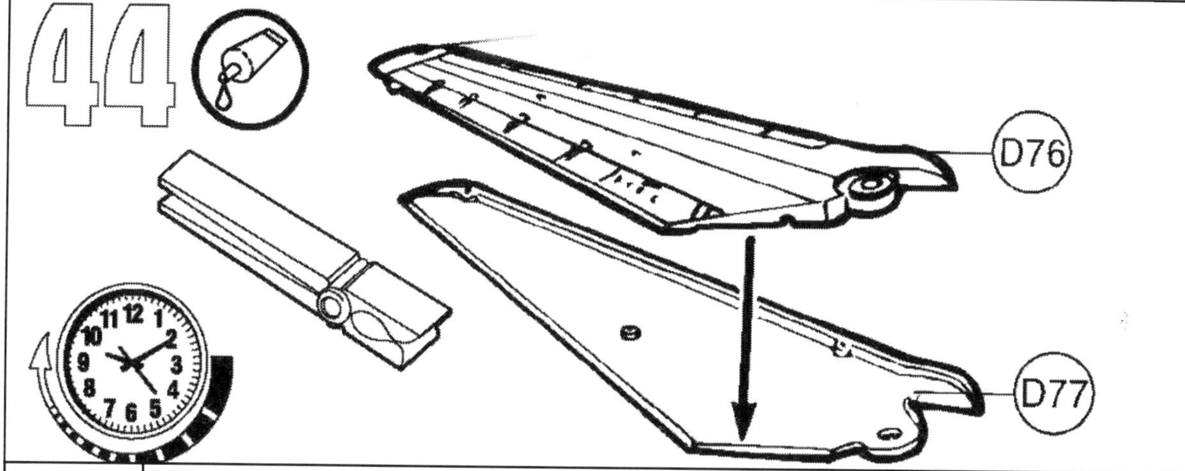 44		**Figure** 55	
358.	Dry fit D76 to D77 as shown in "Figure 55" on page 71	Section 44	
359.	Glue D76 to D77 as shown in "Figure 55" on page 71 This Assembly will be referred to as Assembly 44 in future steps.	Section 44	
M&P = Marking and Painting, O = Optional, Aftermarket in Gray			

Step	Instruction	Source	Done

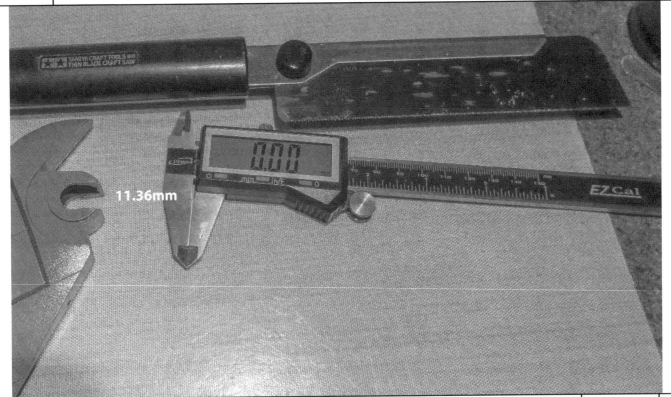

11.36mm

| | I highly recommend cutting a section from the wing so you can work the wing separate from the fuselage. I reviewed the posts on the B-1B Builders Support Group on Facebook and this is a supported modification. I'm going to write the steps in this book assuming that you made this mod. If you don't want to do this, then you may have to jump around the book a bit and paint the fuselage with the wings connected.
Here are the details...
The post in the fuselage is about 11.17mm in diameter
The hole in the wing that slips over the post is 11.95mm in diameter
Make a mark on the hole next to the protruding piece that acts a stop
Measure 11.3mm down on the other side of the hole and made a mark.
Gently clamp the wing in a vise and slowly cut thru the edge with a fine tooth saw and sand down the edges which to make the opening about 11.36mm (see photo)
Do a dry fit on the post in the bottom half of the fuselage and remove
Tape the top and bottom halves of the fuselage together
Attempt to insert the modified wing to the post thru the opening in the fuselage. You may have to jockey it around a bit (spread the opening a hair)
Remove the tape and separate the fuselage halves and remove the wing
Repeat the above steps for the other wing | O | |

M&P = Marking and Painting, O = Optional, Aftermarket in Gray

Step	Instruction	Source	Done

Figure 56

Step	Instruction	Source
360.	Dry fit Assembly 43 to Assembly 42 as shown in "Figure 56" on page 73 (no glue). You should have already done this step if you cut the wings in the previous steps.	Section 44
361.	Dry fit Assembly 44 to Assembly 42 as shown in "Figure 56" on page 73 (no glue). This Assembly will be referred to as Assembly 45 in future steps. You should have already done this step if you cut the wings in the previous steps.	Section 44
362.	Assuming you cut the wings as recommended, we're going to paint the wings along with adding any photo etch and decals and set them aside	M&P

Figure 57

M&P = Marking and Painting, O = Optional, Aftermarket in Gray

Step	Instruction	Source	Done
363.	Make 9 equidistant pencil marks on the trailing edge and tip of the right wing as shown in "Figure 57" on page 73. Using a pin, make a little indentation on each mark	PE 48857	
364.	Glue 27 (9 pcs) to the indentations on the trailing edge and tip of right wing as shown in "Figure 57" on page 73. Also add another drop pf CA for support.	PE 48857	
365.	Make 9 equidistant marks on the trailing edge and tip of the left wing as shown in "Figure 57" on page 73. Using a pin, make a little indentation on each mark	PE 48857	
366.	Glue 27 (9 pcs) to the indentations on the trailing edge and tip of left wing as shown in "Figure 57" on page 73.Also add another drop pf CA for support.	PE 48857	
367.	Sorry to state the obvious, but be careful handling these wings so to not knock off these pieces		
M&P = Marking and Painting, O = Optional, Aftermarket in Gray			

Step	Instruction	Source	Done
	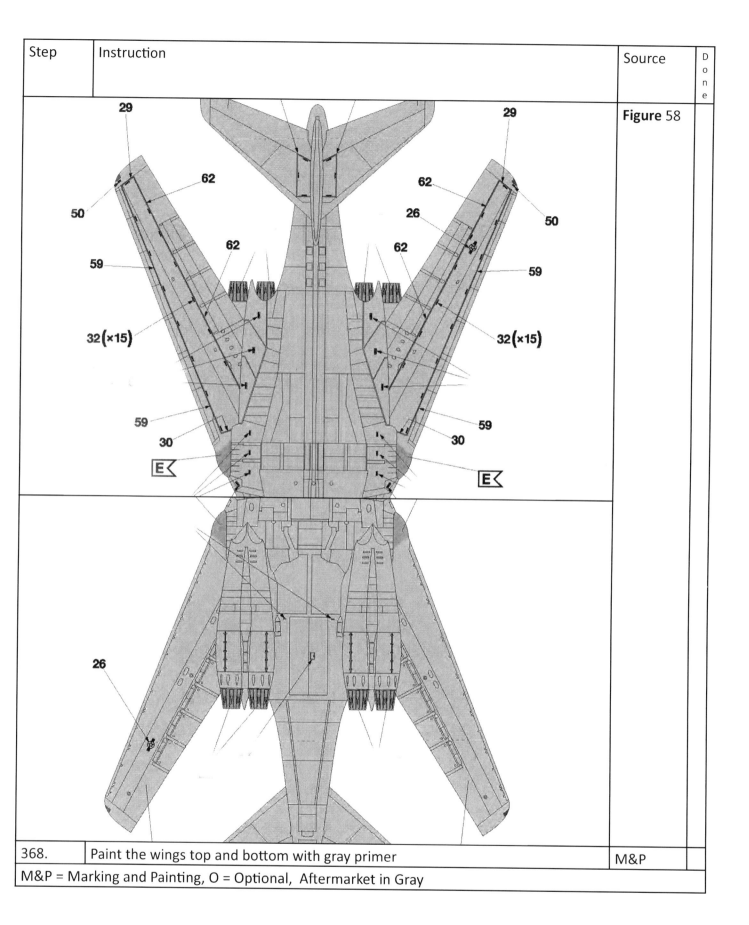	**Figure** 58	
368.	Paint the wings top and bottom with gray primer	M&P	

M&P = Marking and Painting, O = Optional, Aftermarket in Gray

Step	Instruction	Source	Done
369.	As an option ....instead of adding decals 30, 59, 29, and 62 in a later step, you can paint this stripe on the wing instead. Paint the tops of the wings with TS-48 Gunship Gray. Using masking tape 2mm wide, run a border around the top of the wing as shown in "Figure 60" on page 80 or per the photos in Willy Peeter's book	M&P	
370.	Paint the wings top and bottom with TS-99 IJN Gray	M&P	
371.	Mask the wing and paint the areas of the wings butts with TS-67 IJN Gray as shown in "Figure 58" on page 75	M&P	
372.	Paint the wings top and bottom with TS-13 Clear	M&P	
373.	Consider tracing the panel lines with a Micron .005mm black pen	M&P, O	
374.	Apply the following decals to the top of the wings as shown in "Figure 58" on page 75..starting from right front and working around to the left front. (Check them off as you apply them) 30* 59* 32 (x15) 59* 50 29* 62* 26 62* 62* 62* 29* 50 59* 32 (x15) 59* 30* * Skip if you painted the strip in the previous step Apply 26 to the bottom of one wing as shown in "Figure 58" on page 75	M&P	
375.	Paint the wings with two coats of TS-80 Flat Clear and set them aside Next we'll work the fuselage	M&P	

We're at the point where you should decide on how to support this huge model as we assemble the fuselage. In the next few pages I'll show you what I did.

M&P = Marking and Painting, O = Optional, Aftermarket in Gray

Step	Instruction	Source	Done

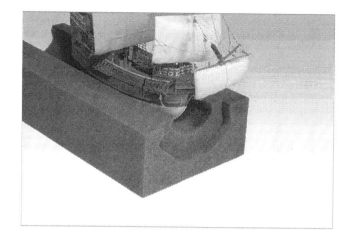

Triple Duty Foam Cradle For Model Ships
Item #: 85819

Our custom-designed Ship Cradle holds your model while you build, decorate or repair. Concave shape holds large scale models and, with the included insert, adapts in seconds to hold small scale models as well. Use the convex shape when you want to work on the entire hull. Safely tip the model in the cradle for access with the superstructure installed. Durable CNC-cut foam rubber holds hulls from 2-3/4 inches to 5-1/2 inches (beam) gently, yet securely. Includes all 3 pieces. Overall size: 7-1/2 inches wide x 3-1/2 inches high x 15 inches long. Convex shape: 3 inches wide.

Micro-Mark sells a foam cradle that works great for the B-1B fuselage. Remove the center section and lay the fuselage upside down to work on the bomb bay doors and landing gear with enough space below as to not damage any small parts on the top. You can just use the foam cradle by itself or you can mount it on a fixture so you can reposition the fuselage and let gravity be your third hand (see next steps).

Simpson Strong-Tie >
20-Gauge 1-1/4 in. x 9 in.
Strap Tie

Overview

Simpson Strong-Tie straps and plates join and reinforce joints with simple, versatile solutions for a wide range of connections. Available in many lengt... See Full Descriptic

PanaVise 337 Fixturing Head
by Panavise

First, you need to mount the foam cradle on a fixture. You'll need a strap tie from Home Depot (Model LSTA9) and a Panavise 337 Fixturing Head (Amazon)

M&P = Marking and Painting, O = Optional, Aftermarket in Gray

Step	Instruction	Source	Done

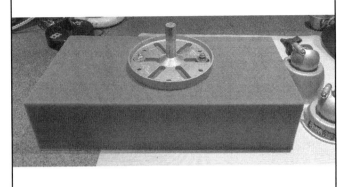

Wrap the edges of the strap with electrical tape so the edges don't cut into the foam. Use 2 machine screws with nuts and poke a hole thru the foam and fasten the fixturing head on the other side

PanaVise 300 Standard Base
by Panavise

PanaVise 312 Tray Base Mount
by Panavise

You'll also need the Panavise 300 Std Base and the Panavise 312 Base Mount (both from Amazon)

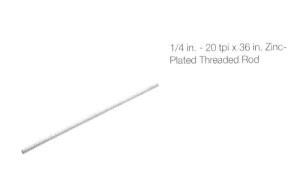

1/4 in. - 20 tpi x 36 in. Zinc-Plated Threaded Rod

M&P = Marking and Painting, O = Optional, Aftermarket in Gray

Step	Instruction	Source	Done

To raise the fixturing head up high so we can position the model vertically, you'll need some threaded rods (Home Depot). Make sure they are 1/4 inch diameter with 20 threads per inch. They come in different lengths. I bought three at 8 inches and three at 12 inches. I got 2 bases and 2 base mounts. Thread a nut on to the bottom of each rod, add a washer and screw them into the base and tighten the nut. Use 2 nuts on the top of each thread to fasten the standard base

 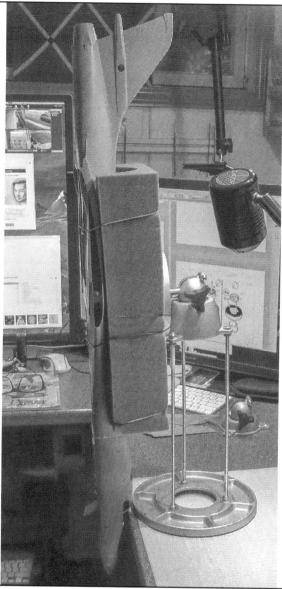

Before setting the base in a vertical position, strap the model to the foam cradle with 2 rubber bands. The rubber bands will not be enough so thread an insulated wire (bare wire may damage the model) thru the wing opening and wrap it around the fixturing head. The left photo shows using the 8 inch stand to attach the cockpit/nose. The right photo shows using the 12 inch stand to attach the tail section. Notice that I had to hang the nose off the edge of the workbench - man this model is huge...Almost 3 ft long.

M&P = Marking and Painting, O = Optional, Aftermarket in Gray

Step	Instruction	Source	Done

Figure 59

Step	Instruction	Source	Done
376.	Dry fit C78 to Assembly 45 as shown in "Figure 59" on page 80 except with no wings	Section 45	
377.	Glue C78 to Assembly 45 as shown in "Figure 59" on page 80 except with no wings. This Assembly will be referred to as Assembly 46 in future steps.	Section 45	

Figure 60

Step	Instruction	Source	Done
378.	Dry fit Assembly 18 to Assembly 51 as shown in "Figure 60" on page 80	Section 67	

M&P = Marking and Painting, O = Optional, Aftermarket in Gray

Step	Instruction	Source	Done
379.	Glue Assembly 18 to Assembly 51 as shown in "Figure 60" on page 80. This Assembly will be referred to as Assembly 67 in future steps.	Section 67	
		Figure 61	
380.	Dry fit D113 to D114 as shown in "Figure 61" on page 81	Section 68	
381.	Glue D113 to D114 as shown in "Figure 61" on page 81 . This Assembly will be referred to as Assembly 68 in future steps. Set this aside for now. We'll paint this separate from the fuselage and add it afterwards.	Section 68	
		Figure 62	
382.	Dry fit D116 to D115 as shown in "Figure 62" on page 81	Section 69	
383.	Glue D116 to D115 as shown in "Figure 62" on page 81. This Assembly will be referred to as Assembly 69 in future steps. Set this aside for now. We'll paint this separate from the fuselage and add it afterwards.	Section 69	
M&P = Marking and Painting, O = Optional, Aftermarket in Gray			

Step	Instruction	Source	Done
	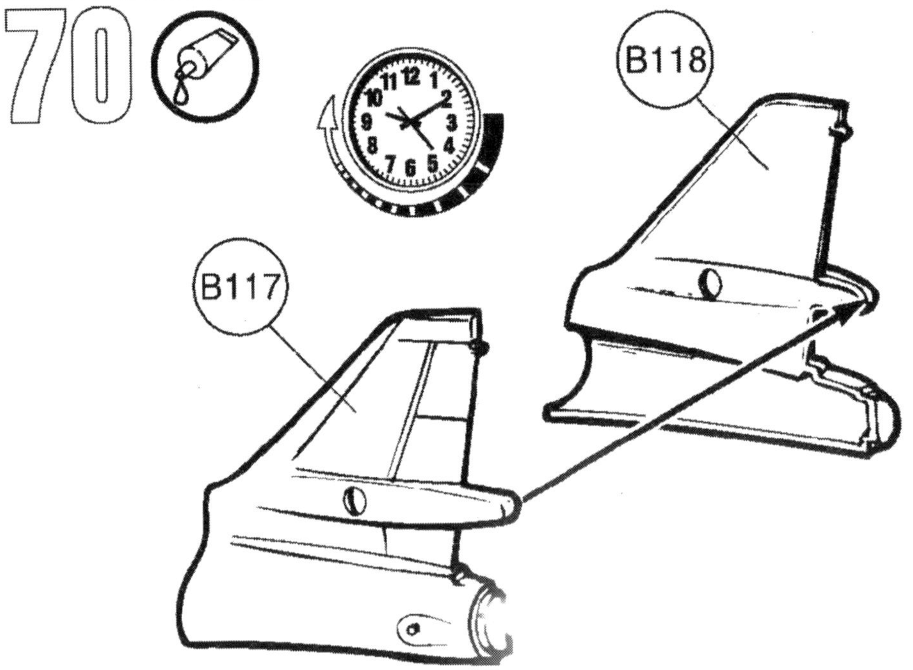 **Figure** 63		
384.	Dry fit B117 to B118 as shown in "Figure 63" on page 82	Section 70	
385.	Glue B117 to B118 as shown in "Figure 63" on page 82	Section 70	
	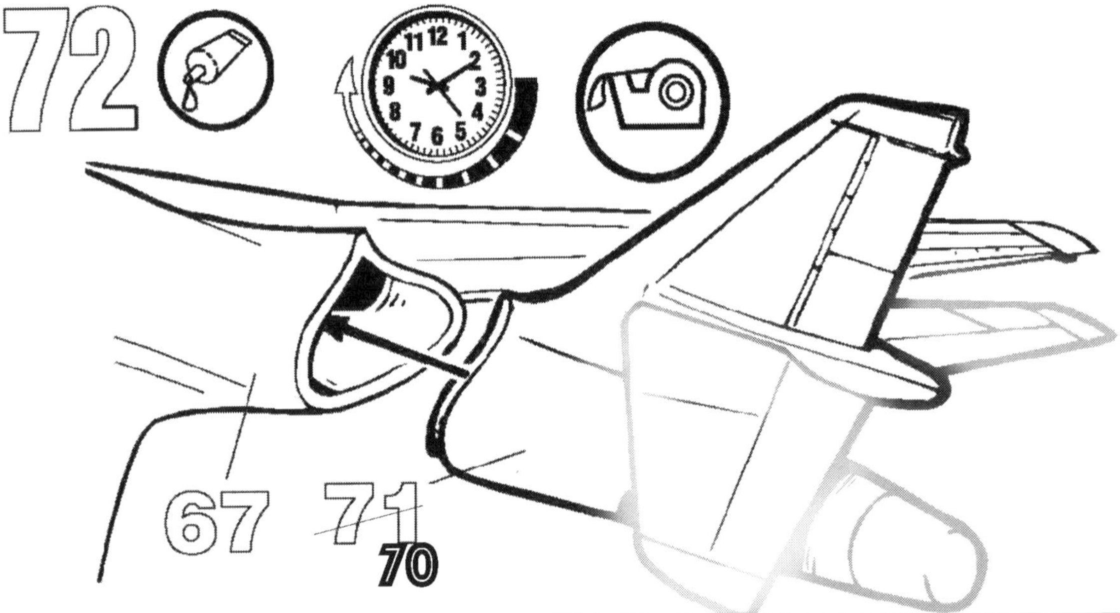 **Figure** 64		
386.	Dry fit Assembly 70 to Assembly 67 as shown in "Figure 64" on page 82	Section 72	
387.	Glue Assembly 70 to Assembly 67 as shown in "Figure 64" on page 82. This Assembly will be referred to as Assembly 72 in future steps.	Section 72	
M&P = Marking and Painting, O = Optional, Aftermarket in Gray			

Step	Instruction	Source	Done
		Figure 65	
388.	Dry fit clear part 121 to Assembly 74 as shown in "Figure 65" on page 83	Section 75	
389.	Glue clear part 121 to Assembly 74 as shown in "Figure 65" on page 83. This Assembly will be referred to as Assembly 75 in future steps.	Section 75	
390.	Apply masking to all clear parts added to the model so far. You can use Eduard's EX 480 Mask Set, New Ware Mask (see next step) or make you own	M&P	
M&P = Marking and Painting, O = Optional, Aftermarket in Gray			

Step	Instruction	Source	D o n e

NWAM0044

1/48 B-1B ADVANCED MASKS

for Revell kit

http://mek.kosmo.cz/newware

1/48 scale

tom.nwkits@seznam.cz

Important:
Let the sprayed color dry before applying masks. Remove masks very carefully after painting.
Where the mask is divided into A and B parts, first apply part A, next part B.
The set does not include masks for all areas, so mask the rest with masking tape or liquid mask.
K kit part
* start placing the mask from this point

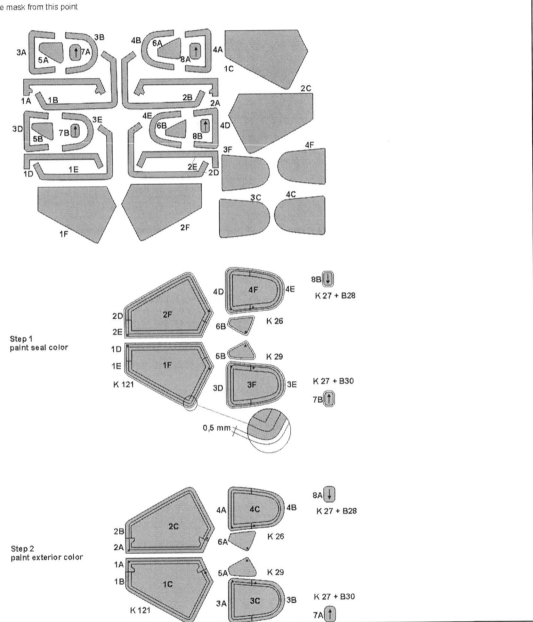

M&P = Marking and Painting, O = Optional, Aftermarket in Gray

Step	Instruction	Source	Done
391.	I highly recommend getting the New Ware Mask for this model. It easily helps you get the white trim around the clear parts. Apply the masks in Step 1 for now. In future steps, we'll paint the model with primer, then paint over and beyond the Step 1 masks with white & flat clear, and finally, we'll replace the Step 1 masks with Step 2 to cover the white trim as we paint the model with the final gray color.	O, M&P	
		Figure 66	
392.	Dry fit B122 to Assembly 75 as shown in "Figure 66" on page 85	Section 76	
393.	If you want the option to remove this panel to display the interior, I recommend applying some Microscale Liquitape to hold it while we paint and assemble the rest of the model...Otherwise, glue B122 to Assembly 75 as shown in "Figure 66" on page 85. This Assembly will be referred to as Assembly 76 in future steps.	Section 65	
M&P = Marking and Painting, O = Optional, Aftermarket in Gray			

Step	Instruction	Source	Done
		Figure 66a	
394.	As an option, you could cut B122 into 3 pieces along the black lines as shown in "Figure 66a" on page 86. Permanently attach the center section to the fuselage. Take note of the hinge marks in the back part of the opening. You could attach the escape hatch doors in an open position. See some of the photos from the Facebook group " B-1B Builder's Support Group" where members Thierry Lavoie and Haagen Klaus did this modification.	O	
395.	We're close to the major paint step. Lets work on the doors. We'll paint the insides and mount them in a closed position while we paint the fuselage (except the nose gear doors)...I'll outline the process in the next few steps. In case you are wondering, we're going to assemble and paint the engines separately in a later section.	M&P	
		Figure 67	

M&P = Marking and Painting, O = Optional, Aftermarket in Gray

Step	Instruction	Source	Done
396.	Paint the insides of B46, B47, B48, C86, C87, C106, C107, C109, and C110 with white primer	M&P	
397.	Paint the insides of B46, B47, B48, C86, C87, C106, C107, C109, and C110 with TS-26 Pure White	M&P	
398.	Set B46, B47, & B48 aside for now because we can't close them.	M&P	
399.	Set C106 and C109 aside for now. We'll have to substitute C128 and C129 to close the wheel well during painting. We'll paint C106 and C109 separately and replace C128 and C129 when we add the landing gear at a later step.	M&P	
400.	Mask the nose gear wheel well (I jammed some soft foam)	M&P	
401.	B2 should already be added in a previous step or at least masked if you had PE.	M&P	
402.	Dry fit and tape together with some styrene strips for support C86, C107, and C129. Apply Microscale Liquitape and set the 3 doors to main landing gear wheel well in a closed position	M&P	
403.	Repeat the steps above with C87, C110, and C128	M&P	
404.	DO NOT ASSEMBLE C111 TO C112 AT THIS TIME Paint C112 (6 pcs) and C111 (24 pcs) with white primer	M&P	
405.	Paint C112 (6 pcs) and C111 (24 pcs with TS-26 Pure White. Set C111 (24 pcs) aside for now.	M&P	
406.	Tape the doors together and dry fit C112 (3 sets) to the weapons bays in a closed position. Using some Microscale Liqui-tape, glue C112 (3 sets) to the weapons bays in a closed position.	M&P	

M&P = Marking and Painting, O = Optional, Aftermarket in Gray

Step	Instruction	Source	Done

648 252 Sniper ATP

1/48

BRASSIN

BRASSIN

eduard

M&P = Marking and Painting, O = Optional, Aftermarket in Gray

Step	Instruction	Source	Done

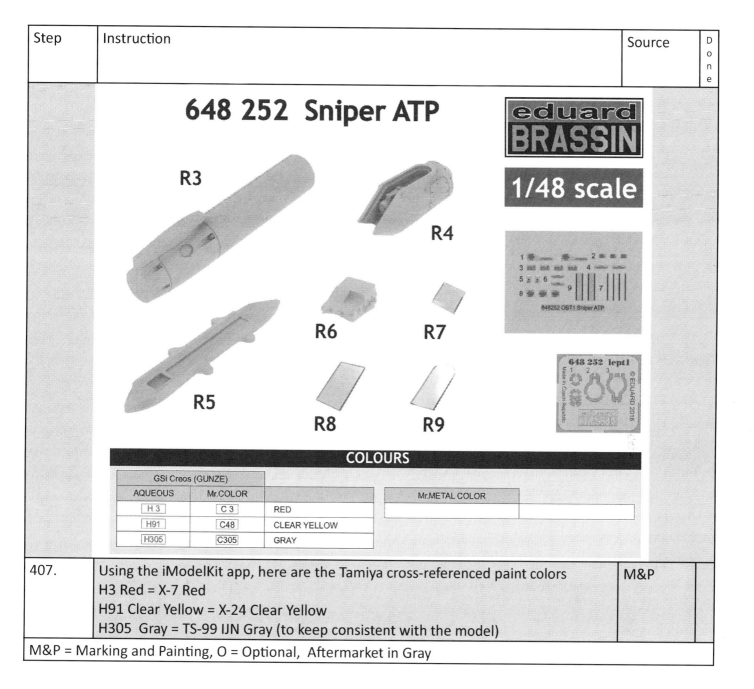

648 252 Sniper ATP

eduard BRASSIN

1/48 scale

R3

R4

R6

R7

R5

R8

R9

648252 OBT1 Sniper ATP

648 252 lept1
© EDUARD 2016

COLOURS

GSI Creos (GUNZE)			Mr.METAL COLOR	
AQUEOUS	Mr.COLOR			
H 3	C 3	RED		
H91	C48	CLEAR YELLOW		
H305	C305	GRAY		

Step	Instruction	Source	Done
407.	Using the iModelKit app, here are the Tamiya cross-referenced paint colors H3 Red = X-7 Red H91 Clear Yellow = X-24 Clear Yellow H305 Gray = TS-99 IJN Gray (to keep consistent with the model)	M&P	

M&P = Marking and Painting, O = Optional, Aftermarket in Gray

Step	Instruction	Source	Done

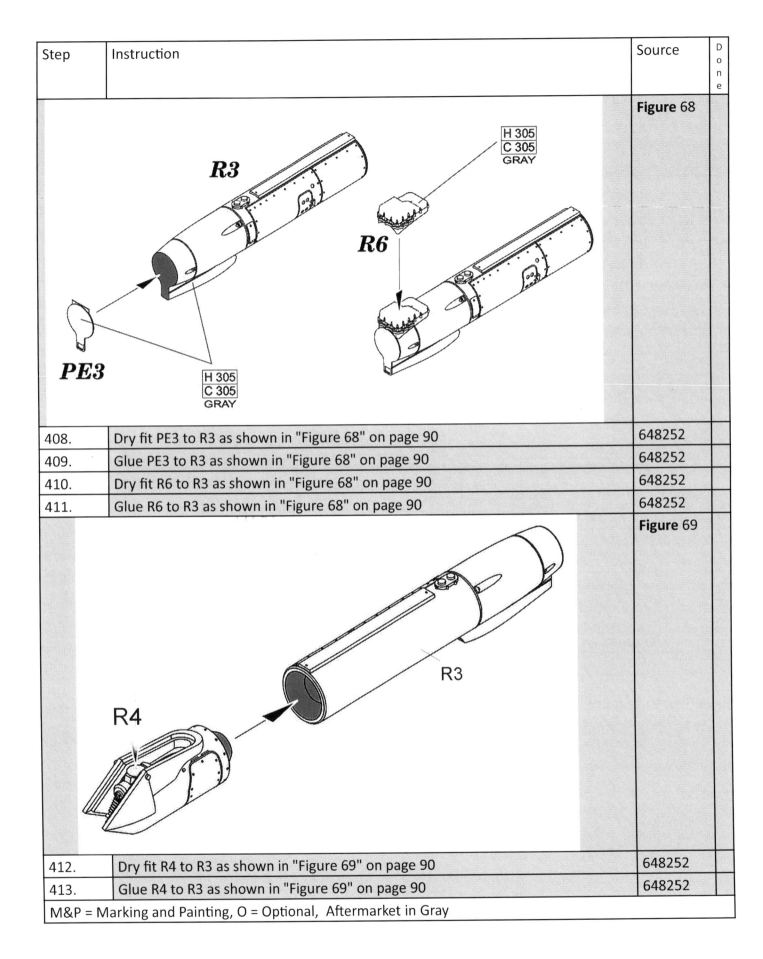

Figure 68

408.	Dry fit PE3 to R3 as shown in "Figure 68" on page 90	648252
409.	Glue PE3 to R3 as shown in "Figure 68" on page 90	648252
410.	Dry fit R6 to R3 as shown in "Figure 68" on page 90	648252
411.	Glue R6 to R3 as shown in "Figure 68" on page 90	648252

Figure 69

412.	Dry fit R4 to R3 as shown in "Figure 69" on page 90	648252
413.	Glue R4 to R3 as shown in "Figure 69" on page 90	648252

M&P = Marking and Painting, O = Optional, Aftermarket in Gray

Step	Instruction	Source	Done
	Figure 70 PE4 ↲ PE4 ↲ H 305 / C 305 GRAY R3 H 305 / C 305 GRAY		
414.	Form and dry fit PE4 (2pcs) on either side of R3as shown in "Figure 70" on page 91	648252	
415.	Glue PE4 (2pcs) on either side of R3 as shown in "Figure 70" on page 91	648252	
416.	Paint the R3 assembly and R5 with gray primer	M&P	
417.	Paint the R3 assembly and R5 with TS-99 IJN Gray	M&P	
418.	Paint the R3 assembly with TS-13 Clear	M&P	
M&P = Marking and Painting, O = Optional, Aftermarket in Gray			

Step	Instruction	Source	Done
		Figure 71	

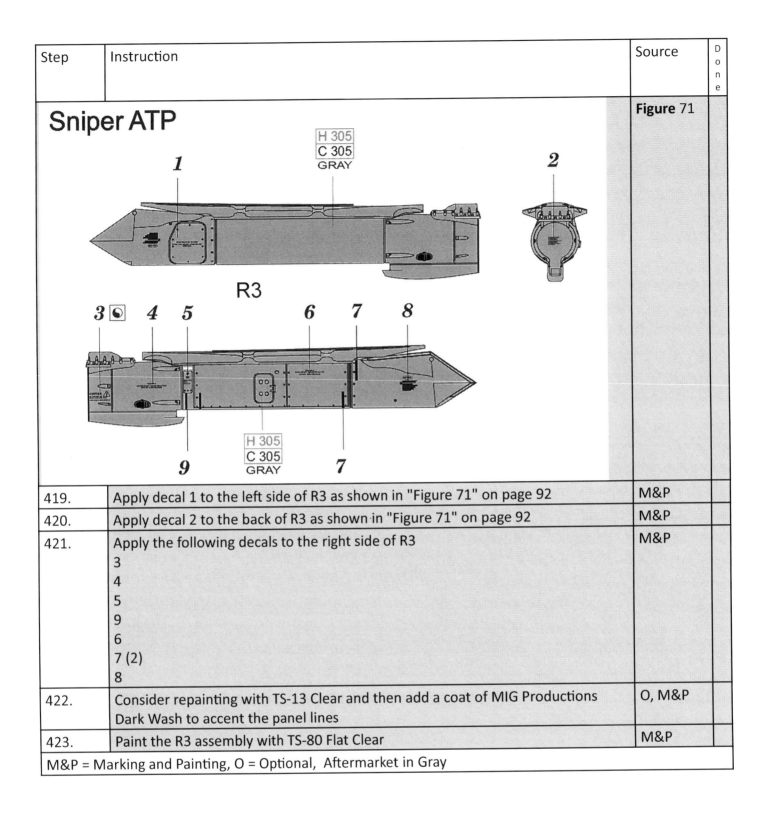

419.	Apply decal 1 to the left side of R3 as shown in "Figure 71" on page 92	M&P	
420.	Apply decal 2 to the back of R3 as shown in "Figure 71" on page 92	M&P	
421.	Apply the following decals to the right side of R3 3 4 5 9 6 7 (2) 8	M&P	
422.	Consider repainting with TS-13 Clear and then add a coat of MIG Productions Dark Wash to accent the panel lines	O, M&P	
423.	Paint the R3 assembly with TS-80 Flat Clear	M&P	
M&P = Marking and Painting, O = Optional, Aftermarket in Gray			

Step	Instruction	Source	Done
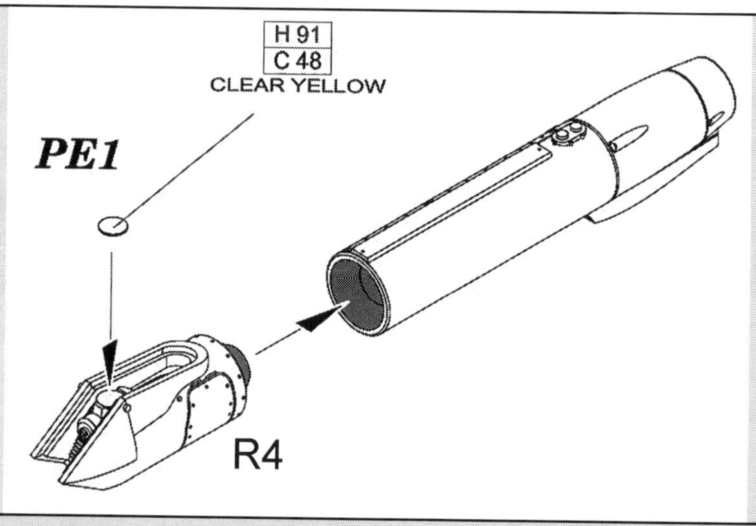	Figure 72	**Figure** 72	
424.	Paint PE1 with X-24 Clear Yellow	M&P	
425.	Dry fit PE1 with R4 as shown in "Figure 72" on page 93	648252	
426.	Glue PE1 with R4 as shown in "Figure 72" on page 93	648252	
	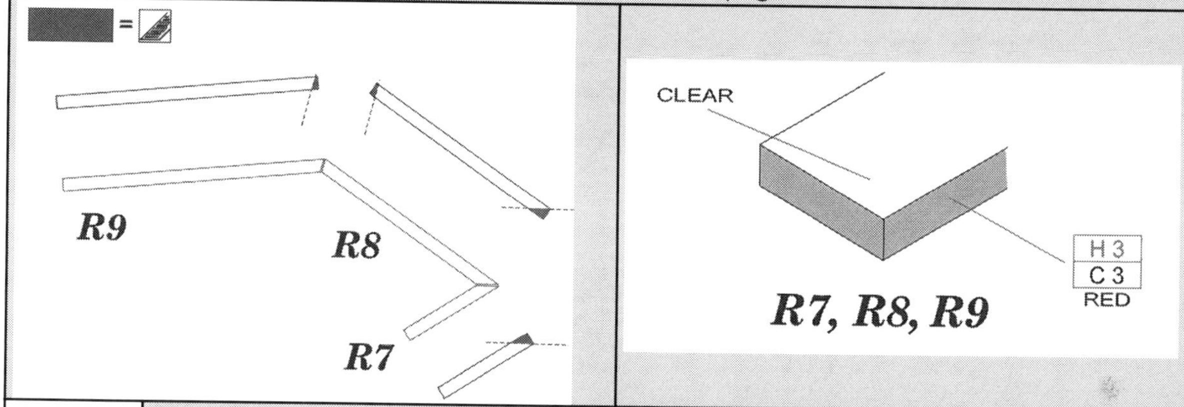	**Figure** 73	
427.	Trim R7, R8, and R9 as shown in "Figure 73" on page 93	648252	
428.	Paint the edges of R7, R8, & R9 with X-7 Red as shown in "Figure 73" on page 93	M&P	
M&P = Marking and Painting, O = Optional, Aftermarket in Gray			

Step	Instruction	Source	Done
		Figure 74	

Step	Instruction	Source	Done
429.	Dry fit R9 to R4 as shown in "Figure 74" on page 94	648252	
430.	Glue R9 to R4 as shown in "Figure 74" on page 94	648252	
431.	Dry fit R7 to R4 as shown in "Figure 74" on page 94	648252	
432.	Glue R7 to R4 as shown in "Figure 74" on page 94	648252	
433.	Dry fit R8 to R4 as shown in "Figure 74" on page 94	648252	
434.	Glue R8 to R4 as shown in "Figure 74" on page 94	648252	
M&P = Marking and Painting, O = Optional, Aftermarket in Gray			

Step	Instruction	Source	Done
		Figure 75	

R5

H 305
C 305
GRAY

R3

| 435. | Dry fit R5 to R3 as shown in "Figure 75" on page 95 | 648252 | |
| 436. | Glue R5 to R3 as shown in "Figure 75" on page 95 | 648252 | |

M&P = Marking and Painting, O = Optional, Aftermarket in Gray

Step	Instruction	Source	Done
		Figure 76	

SHAPEWAYS

MARKETPLACE > MINIATURES > AIRCRAFT >

1:48 Scale Pylon for B-1B Sniper Pod
Made by BaconFistModels

$7.00

Smooth Fine Detail Plastic

3D printed in matte translucent plastic that showcases fine and intricate details.

QTY 1 ▼   BUY NOW

DIGITAL PREVIEW
Not a Photo

Smooth Fine Detail Plastic

Sniper Pod Pylon Location

Step	Instruction	Source	Done
437.	Dry fit R5 to the Pylon. Remove the Sniper Pod assembly and set aside for now. We'll add this later	Shapeways	
438.	Dry fit the Pylon to the spot as shown in "Figure 76" on page 96	Shapeways	
439.	Glue the Pylon to the spot as shown in "Figure 76" on page 96 and the photo below from Military.com	Shapeways	
M&P = Marking and Painting, O = Optional, Aftermarket in Gray			

Step	Instruction	Source	Done

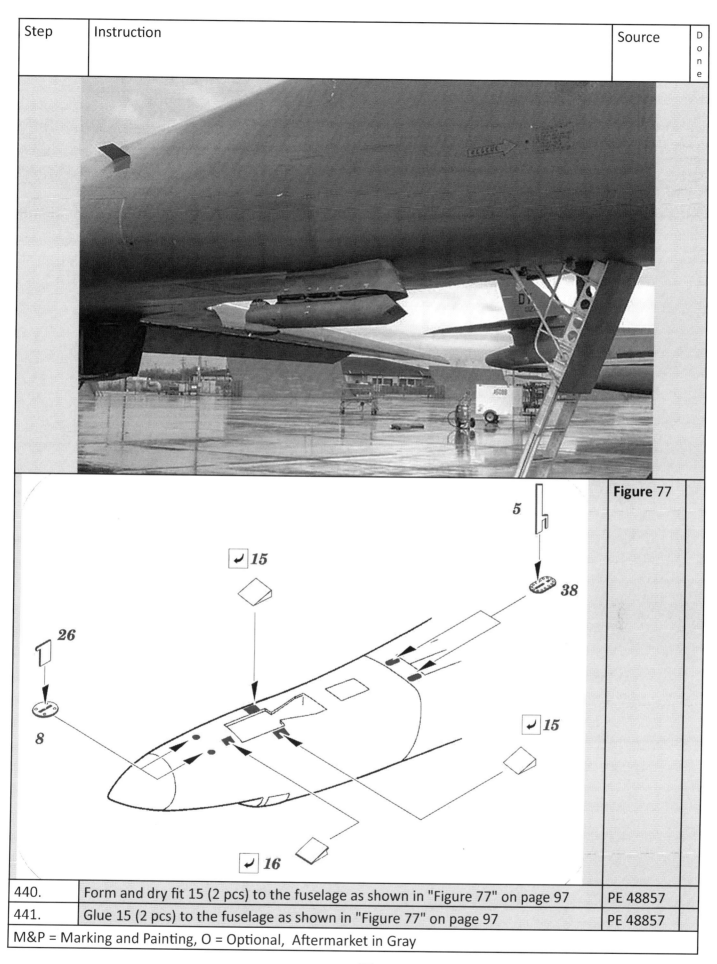

Figure 77

Step	Instruction	Source	Done
440.	Form and dry fit 15 (2 pcs) to the fuselage as shown in "Figure 77" on page 97	PE 48857	
441.	Glue 15 (2 pcs) to the fuselage as shown in "Figure 77" on page 97	PE 48857	
M&P = Marking and Painting, O = Optional, Aftermarket in Gray			

Step	Instruction	Source	Done
442.	Form and dry fit 16 to the fuselage as shown in "Figure 77" on page 97	PE 48857	
443.	Glue 16 to the fuselage as shown in "Figure 77" on page 97	PE 48857	
444.	Dry fit 8 (2 pcs) to the fuselage as shown in "Figure 77" on page 97	PE 48857	
445.	Glue 8 (2 pcs) to the fuselage as shown in "Figure 77" on page 97	PE 48857	
446.	Glue 26 (2pcs) to 8 as shown in "Figure 77" on page 97	PE 48857	
447.	Dry fit 38 (2 pcs) to the fuselage as shown in "Figure 77" on page 97	PE 48857	
448.	Glue 38 (2 pcs) to the fuselage as shown in "Figure 77" on page 97	PE 48857	
449.	Glue 5 (2pcs) to 38 as shown in "Figure 77" on page 97	PE 48857	
		Figure 78	
450.	**You can skip all steps with this figure if you added these parts with Barracuda**	O	
451.	Dry fit 13 to the tail section as shown in "Figure 78" on page 98	PE 48857	
452.	Glue 13 to the tail section as shown in "Figure 78" on page 98	PE 48857	
453.	Glue 23 to 13 as shown in "Figure 78" on page 98	PE 48857	
454.	Dry fit 14 to the tail section as shown in "Figure 78" on page 98	PE 48857	
455.	Glue 14 to the tail section as shown in "Figure 78" on page 98	PE 48857	
456.	Glue 40 to 14 as shown in "Figure 78" on page 98	PE 48857	
M&P = Marking and Painting, O = Optional, Aftermarket in Gray			

Step	Instruction	Source	Done

BR48239

B-1B External
Upgrade Set

Designed for the 1/48 Revell
B-1B Lancer to allow building
late production aircraft.

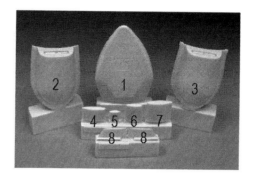

This set contains a number of antennas and fairings to allow you to model a later production Lancer. The Revell kit, as kitted only allows building of the early Bone, before the many upgrades were installed. This set supplies parts for the towed array fairings, early & late DAS antennas as well as a few electronics antennas. This set should be paired with BR 48237 8-1 B Late Exhausts - No Turkey Feathers.

		Figure 79	

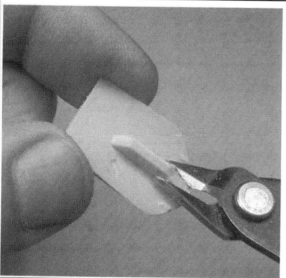 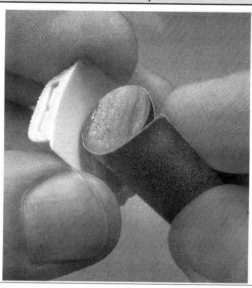

| 457. | These antennas are for the late model. If you just want to show the earlier model, add antennas 4 thru 7 as shown in "Figure 81" on page 101. I decided to add the later model antennas.
Begin by sawing the two towed array fairings (2,3) and the late DAS fairing (1) from the mold blocks. Remove the casting ribs with nippers as shown in "Figure 79" on page 99. Grind or sand away the remaining rib until smooth. | BR48239 | |

M&P = Marking and Painting, O = Optional, Aftermarket in Gray

Step	Instruction	Source	Done
		Figure 80	
458.	Test fit and adjust. Attach the towed array fairings in the position as shown in "Figure 80" on page 100 with super glue (CA). Install the DAS late fairing (if fitted) with CA or 5 minute epoxy to the sides and bottom of the tail section B117 and B118. There are no hard and fast rules about what aircraft was fitted with what modifications at any certain time. Study photos of the aircraft you are building to help determine the mods applicable to your model.	BR48239	
M&P = Marking and Painting, O = Optional, Aftermarket in Gray			

Step	Instruction	Source	Done
		Figure 81	
459.	According to Willy Peeter's book on page 19, the antennas numbered 4,5,6 and 7 are for an earlier DAS Defensive Avionics System. You can optionally add these instead of the later DAS antennas in the previous steps. These are molded with a pin on the base to locate it. You can either use this pin or cut it off, sand the base flush, then drill and install your own pin from brass or plastic rod. Note the location of these 4 antenna on the belly as shown in "Figure 81" on page 101. Mark position. Drill a mounting hole, then attach antennas with CA or epoxy during final assembly to prevent breakage.	BR48239	
M&P = Marking and Painting, O = Optional, Aftermarket in Gray			

Step	Instruction	Source	D o n e

	Now we're ready to work on the topside items so I made adjustments to the foam cradle to not touch the PE antennas and flipped the model upright.		
	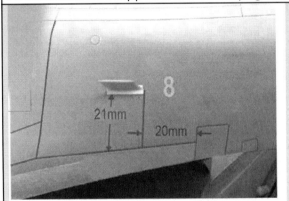 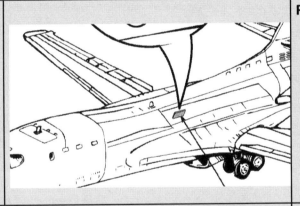	**Figure** 82	
460.	Carefully saw the 2 AN/ALQ-161 ECM antennas (8, 8) from the block. Cleanup and attach as shown in "Figure 82" on page 102. Antennas sit at 45 degree angle when viewed head on each side of the fuselage.	BR48239	
M&P = Marking and Painting, O = Optional, Aftermarket in Gray			

Step	Instruction	Source	D o n e

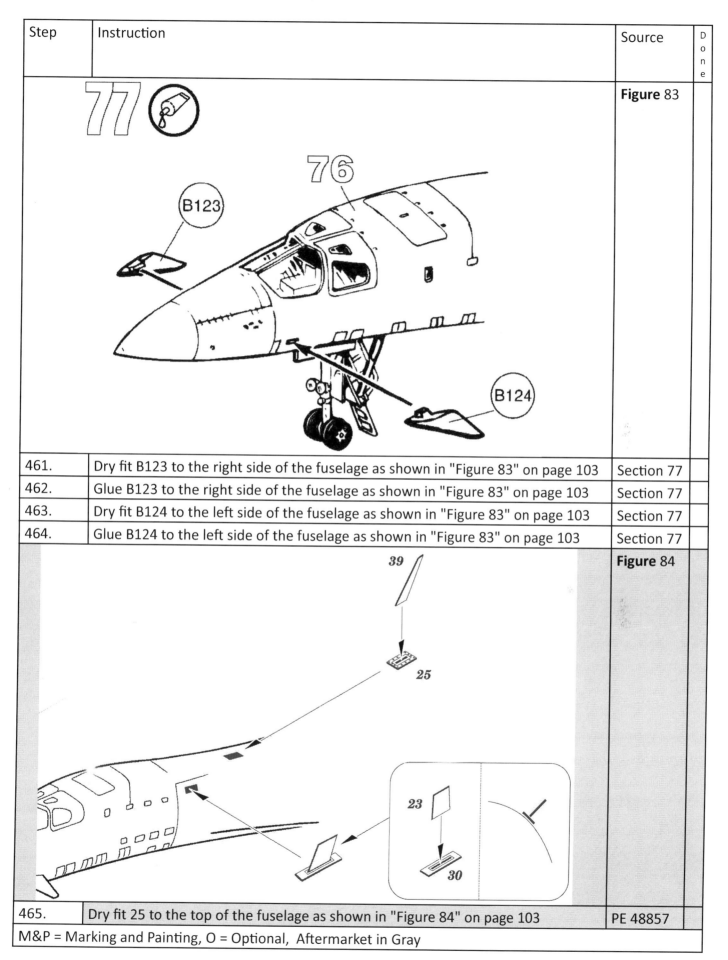

Figure 83

461.	Dry fit B123 to the right side of the fuselage as shown in "Figure 83" on page 103	Section 77	
462.	Glue B123 to the right side of the fuselage as shown in "Figure 83" on page 103	Section 77	
463.	Dry fit B124 to the left side of the fuselage as shown in "Figure 83" on page 103	Section 77	
464.	Glue B124 to the left side of the fuselage as shown in "Figure 83" on page 103	Section 77	

Figure 84

465.	Dry fit 25 to the top of the fuselage as shown in "Figure 84" on page 103	PE 48857	

M&P = Marking and Painting, O = Optional, Aftermarket in Gray

Step	Instruction	Source	Done
466.	Glue 25 to the top of the fuselage as shown in "Figure 84" on page 103	PE 48857	
467.	Glue 39 to 25 as shown in "Figure 84" on page 103	PE 48857	
468.	Dry fit 30 to the top right side of the fuselage as shown in "Figure 84" on page 103 **(skip if you have Barracuda)**	PE 48857	
469.	Glue 30 to the top right side of the fuselage as shown in "Figure 84" on page 103 **(skip if you have Barracuda)**	PE 48857	
470.	Glue 23 to 30 on the top right side of the fuselage as shown in "Figure 84" on page 103 **(skip if you have Barracuda)**	PE 48857	
471.	Dry fit 30 to the same spot on the left side of the fuselage **(skip if you have Barracuda)**	PE 48857	
472.	Glue 30 to the same spot on the left side of the fuselage **(skip if you have Barracuda)**	PE 48857	
473.	Glue 23 to 30 on the left side of the fuselage **(skip if you have Barracuda)**	PE 48857	
		Figure 85	

M&P = Marking and Painting, O = Optional, Aftermarket in Gray

Step	Instruction	Source	D o n e
474.	Dry fit 42 to the top of the fuselage as shown in "Figure 85" on page 104. I choose to use the kit part A126 instead.	PE 48857	
475.	Glue 42 to the top of the fuselage as shown in "Figure 85" on page 104	PE 48857	
476.	On the left side, measure 4mm up from the hole, make a pencil mark, measure 4mm down from the hole and make a pencil mark	PE 48857	
477.	Glue 49 (3 pcs) over the hole and the two marks on the left side of the fuselage as shown in "Figure 85" on page 104	PE 48857	
478.	Glue 44 (3 pcs) to each 49 on the left side of the fuselage as shown in "Figure 85" on page 104. Put an extra drop of glue for support.	PE 48857	
479.	Dry fit 49 (3 pcs) to the same spots on the right side of the fuselage	PE 48857	
480.	Glue 49 (3 pcs) to the same spots on the right side of the fuselage	PE 48857	
481.	Glue 44 (3 pcs) to each 49 on the right side of the fuselage. Put an extra drop of glue for support.	PE 48857	

Figure 86

M&P = Marking and Painting, O = Optional, Aftermarket in Gray

Step	Instruction	Source	Done
482.	Parts 31 & 32 are called vortex generators. They decrease the turbulence around the tail. Earlier models had 10 (3 on the tail & 7 on the fuselage a little further back in 1 row). Eduard shows adding 9 sets but they actually have 10 sets on the fret so consider adding 10. Later models have 11. See pictures in Daco Publications.	O	
483.	Using a pencil, mark the places on the left side of the aircraft where we'll place the 32's as shown in "Figure 86" on page 105	PE 48857	
484.	Here's what I did.... • Cut the 31's from the fret and leave the 32's on the fret • Put a drop of CA on a plastic plate or styrene. I always use VMS CA for PE • Since these parts are really small, I wear a pair of reading glasses that are 8x • Pick up one 31 with some tweezers, dip it in the drop of CA, and place it in the slot on one of the 32's in the fret. Be careful not to get them in cockeyed. • Repeat this process for all of the 31's • Put a drop of VMS XT Thin CA on plastic plate or styrene and using a pin, put a couple small drops on each 31/32. • After the glue totally sets, carefully cut the 32's from the fret • Helpful tip: keep a little jar with about a 1/4 inch of debonder. After placing a 31 on a 32, dip your tweezers in the debonder and wipe clean. I recommend this whenever using tweezers to dip a part in CA and place on a model.	PE 48857	
485.	Glue 32 (10 pcs) to the pencil marks on the left side of the aircraft as shown in "Figure 86" on page 105	PE 48857	
486.	Using a pencil, mark the places on the right side of the aircraft where we'll place the 32's as shown in "Figure 86" on page 105	PE 48857	
487.	Repeat the process above to attach the 31's to the 32's while still in the fret	PE 48857	
488.	Glue 32 (10 pcs) to the pencil marks on the right side of the aircraft as shown in "Figure 86" on page 105	PE 48857	
489.	Using a pencil, make 3 equally spaced marks on the outer trailing edge of the right horizontal stabilizer as shown in "Figure 86" on page 105	PE 48857	
490.	Using a pin, make holes in each of the pencil marks	PE 48857	
491.	Glue 27 (3 pcs) to the holes in the right trailing edge of the horizontal stabilizer as shown in "Figure 86" on page 105. Put another drop of CA for support.	PE 48857	
492.	Using a pencil, make 3 equally spaced marks on the outer trailing edge of the left horizontal stabilizer as shown in "Figure 86" on page 105	PE 48857	
493.	Using a pin, make holes in each of the pencil marks	PE 48857	
494.	Glue 27 (3 pcs) to the holes on the left trailing edge of the horizontal stabilizer as shown in "Figure 86" on page 105. Put another drop of CA for support.	PE 48857	
495.	Using a pencil, make 3 equally spaced marks on the rudder edge as shown in "Figure 86" on page 105	PE 48857	
496.	Using a pin, make holes in each of the pencil marks	PE 48857	

M&P = Marking and Painting, O = Optional, Aftermarket in Gray

Step	Instruction	Source	Done
497.	Glue 27 (3 pcs) to the holes in rudder as shown in "Figure 86" on page 105. Put another drop of CA for support.	PE 48857	
498.	Using a pencil, make a mark on the top of the tail as shown in "Figure 86" on page 105	PE 48857	
499.	Using a pin, make a holes the pencil mark	PE 48857	
500.	Glue 27 to hole in the top of the tail as shown in "Figure 86" on page 105. Put another drop of CA for support.	PE 48857	

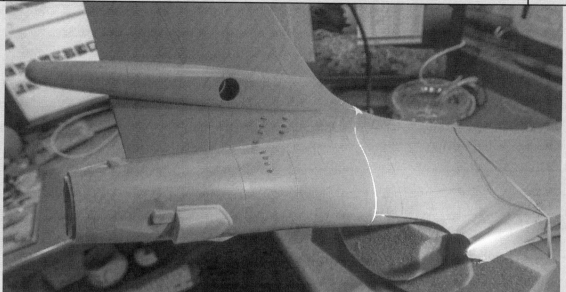

I used the ten 31/32 in the PE set and made an 11th by cutting a couple small pieces from the fret. This configuration is shown in Willy Peeters' book on pages 20 and 21 which also shows the later DAS antennas. By having the fuselage mounted on this foam cradle - Panavise platform, you can tilt the model on it's side to let gravity help you place these small parts. CAUTION: I should have moved the PE group on my model about 10mm further back.

M&P = Marking and Painting, O = Optional, Aftermarket in Gray

Step	Instruction	Source	Done
	Figure 87	**Figure** 87	
501.	**Skip all steps with this figure if you have PE**	O	
502.	Dry fit A126 (2 pcs) to the top of the fuselage as shown in "Figure 87" on page 108	Section 87	
503.	Glue A126 (2 pcs) to the top of the fuselage as shown in "Figure 87" on page 108	Section 87	
		Figure 88	
504.	**Skip all steps with this figure if you have PE**	O	
505.	Dry fit B125 (2 pcs) on each side of the fuselage as shown in "Figure 88" on page 108	Section 86	
506.	Glue B125 (2 pcs) on each side of the fuselage as shown in "Figure 88" on page 108	Section 86	
M&P = Marking and Painting, O = Optional, Aftermarket in Gray			

Step	Instruction	Source	Done
	Figure 89	**Figure** 89	
507.	**Skip all steps with this figure if you have PE or Barracuda**	O	
508.	Cut 2 of the numbered tabs from an empty sprue and trim them to be 7mm x 5mm	Section 89	
509.	Dry fit them on each side of the top of the fuselage as shown in "Figure 89" on page 109	Section 89	
510.	Glue them on each side of the top of the fuselage as shown in "Figure 89" on page 109	Section 89	
M&P = Marking and Painting, O = Optional, Aftermarket in Gray			

Step	Instruction	Source	Done
		Figure 90	

511.	**Skip all steps with this figure if you have PE**	O	
512.	These tabs are called vortex generators. The decrease the turbulence around the tail. According to pictures in Daco Publications, the B-1B only has 11 not 12 as depicted by Revell. To be accurate, omit the lowest one.	O	
513.	Cut 22 of the numbered tabs from an empty sprue and trim them to be 5mm x 2.5mm	Section 89	
514.	Dry fit 11 tabs on the left side of the tail/fuselage as shown in "Figure 90" on page 110	Section 89	
515.	Glue 11 tabs on the left side of the tail/fuselage as shown in "Figure 90" on page 110	Section 89	
516.	Dry fit 11 tabs on the right side of the tail/fuselage in the same spot as the left side	Section 89	
517.	Glue 11 tabs on the right side of the tail/fuselage in the same spot as the left side	Section 89	
M&P = Marking and Painting, O = Optional, Aftermarket in Gray			

Step	Instruction	Source	Done
		Figure 91	

518.	Dry fit B127 to the right side of the fuselage (no glue) as shown in "Figure 91" on page 111	Section 88	
519.	Dry fit B128 to the left side of the fuselage (no glue) as shown in "Figure 91" on page 111	Section 88	
520.	Remove both B127 & B128. We'll paint these separate from the rest of the model.	M&P	

M&P = Marking and Painting, O = Optional, Aftermarket in Gray

Step	Instruction	Source	D o n e

	In the next steps, we'll be painting the fuselage. Normally, I apply paint in my 30 inch paint booth but not with this monster. I removed the inner sections of the cradle and wrapped it & the base in aluminum foil, put it on a 7.5 inch turntable, and then placed it on a cart covered with a trash bag. I wheeled it over to the big exhaust fan in my paint area. I also turn on the exhaust fans in the nearby booth to really exhaust the fumes. I can spin the fuselage around on the turntable.		
	M&P = Marking and Painting, O = Optional, Aftermarket in Gray		

Step	Instruction	Source	Done
		Figure 92	

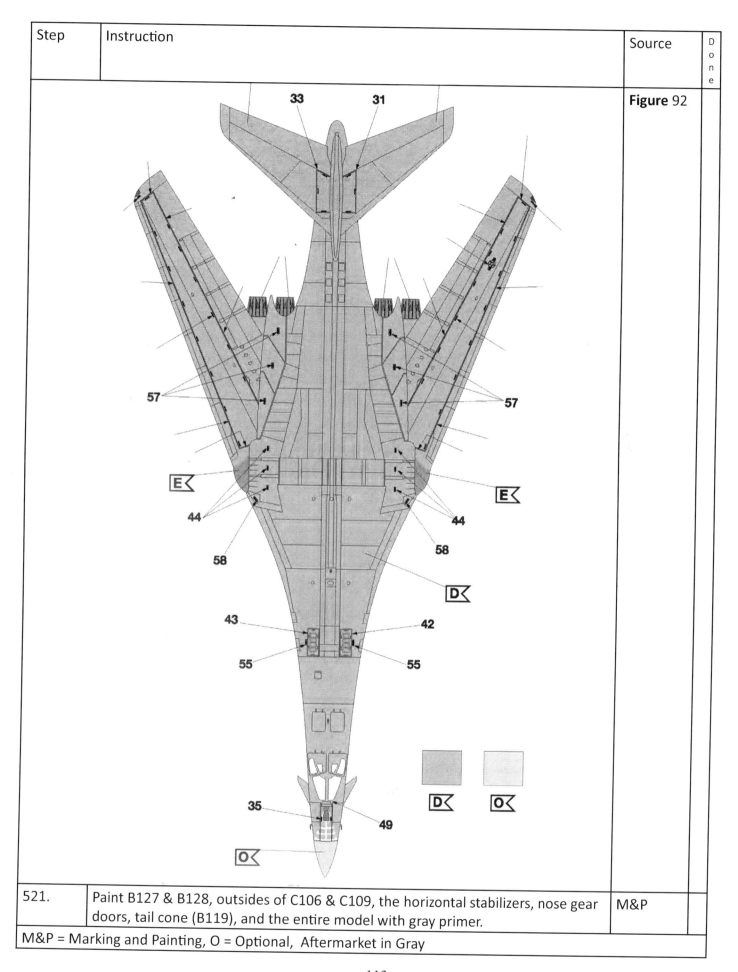

Step	Instruction	Source	Done
521.	Paint B127 & B128, outsides of C106 & C109, the horizontal stabilizers, nose gear doors, tail cone (B119), and the entire model with gray primer.	M&P	

M&P = Marking and Painting, O = Optional, Aftermarket in Gray

Step	Instruction	Source	D o n e
	NWAM0044 1/48 B-1B ADVANCED MASKS for Revell kit http://mek.kosmo.cz/newware tom.nwkits@seznam.cz	1/48 scale	
	Important: Let the sprayed color dry before applying masks. Remove masks very carefully after painting. Where the mask is divided into A and B parts, first apply part A, next part B. The set does not include masks for all areas, so mask the rest with masking tape or liquid mask. K kit part * start placing the mask from this point 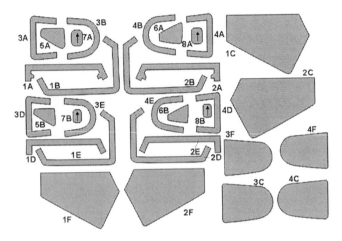 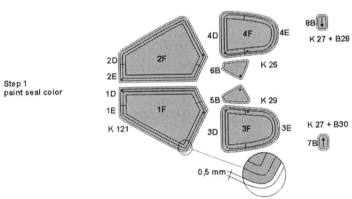 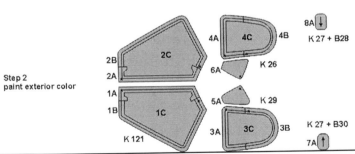		
522.	If you applied Step 1 of the New Ware Mask, paint the outer edges of the clear parts with TS-26 Pure White or X-2 White.	O, M&P	
523.	Remove the Step 1 masks and apply the Step 2 masks	O, M&P	
M&P = Marking and Painting, O = Optional, Aftermarket in Gray			

Step	Instruction	Source	Done
524.	Paint B127 & B128, outsides of C106 & C109, the horizontal stabilizers, nose gear doors, and the entire model with TS-99 IJN Gray. If you used a foam cradle, change the aluminum foil because the primer tends to leave a light power behind.	M&P	
525.	Remove the nose cone and paint the nose cone and tail cone (B119) with TS-82 Black Rubber	M&P	
526.	Paint B127 & B128, the horizontal stabilizers, nose gear doors, and the entire model (including the nose cone) with TS-13 Clear	M&P	
527.	Apply the following decals to the top of the model as shown in "Figure 92" on page 113..starting from right front and working around to the left front. (Check them off as you apply them) 		49
	42
	55
	58
	44 (x3)
	57 (x3)
	31*
	33*
	57 (x3)
	44 (x3)
	58
	43
	55
	35 | * Apply this to the horizontal stabilizers which we have not added to the fuselage yet	M&P	

M&P = Marking and Painting, O = Optional, Aftermarket in Gray

Step	Instruction	Source	Done
		Figure 93	

M&P = Marking and Painting, O = Optional, Aftermarket in Gray

Step	Instruction	Source	Done
528.	Apply the following decals to the bottom of the model as shown in "Figure 93" on page 116. Starting from the top right of Figure 105 and working around to the top left of Figure 105. (Check them off as you apply them) 		34 (x4)
	63
	47
	46
	64
	45 (x2)
	64 (x3)
	46
	47
	63
	53		M&P	

Rockwell B-1B Lancer, 77 Weapons Squadron, USAF Weapons School
Dyess AFB, Texas, October 2012

Figure 94

M&P = Marking and Painting, O = Optional, Aftermarket in Gray

Step	Instruction	Source	Done
529.	I elected to go with the 77 Weapon's Squadron for my build. Apply the following decals to the right side of the model starting on the front as shown in "Figure 94" on page 117. (Check them off as you apply them)	M&P	

	6 *
	4
	10
	5
	13
	56
	60
	52
	26
	54
	3
	2
	1
	15
	16
	56

* Apply this to the nose gear doors which we have not added yet

Figure 95

M&P = Marking and Painting, O = Optional, Aftermarket in Gray

Step	Instruction	Source	Done
530.	Apply the following decals to the left side of the model starting on the front as shown in "Figure 95" on page 118 (Check them off as you apply them) <table><tr><td></td><td>27 *</td></tr><tr><td></td><td>4</td></tr><tr><td></td><td>14</td></tr><tr><td></td><td>60</td></tr><tr><td></td><td>56</td></tr><tr><td></td><td>51</td></tr><tr><td></td><td>26</td></tr><tr><td></td><td>54</td></tr><tr><td></td><td>9</td></tr><tr><td></td><td>11j</td></tr><tr><td></td><td>8</td></tr><tr><td></td><td>17</td></tr><tr><td></td><td>58</td></tr></table> * Apply this to the nose cone which we have not added yet	M&P	
531.	Paint the horizontal stabilizers, nose gear doors, and the entire model with two coats of TS-80 Flat Clear. Now you can remove any canopy masks. Next we'll work the engine, landing gear, and adding the nose & tail cones along with the horizontal stabilizers	M&P	
532.		If you have the Furball Canopy Framing Set 48-043... Apply the decals to the outer edges of the clear parts	O, M&P	
M&P = Marking and Painting, O = Optional, Aftermarket in Gray			

Step	Instruction	Source	Done
		Figure 96	
533.	Dry fit Assembly 17 to the nose as shown in "Figure 96" on page 120	Section 18	
534.	Glue Assembly 17 to the nose as shown in "Figure 96" on page 120	Section 18	
535.	Dry fit B33 to the fuselage as shown in "Figure 96" on page 120 (no glue)	Section 18	
		Figure 97	
536.	Dry fit B119 to the tail section as shown in "Figure 97" on page 120	Section 71	
537.	Glue B119 to the tail section as shown in "Figure 97" on page 120	Section 71	
538.	Dry fit Assembly 68 thru the tail section as shown in "Figure 97" on page 120	Section 71	
539.	Dry fit Assembly 69 to Assembly 68 as shown in "Figure 97" on page 120	Section 71	
540.	Glue Assembly 69 to Assembly 68 as shown in "Figure 97" on page 120. They say not to glue these to the fuselage but I elected to do that because they would always tip back.	Section 71	
M&P = Marking and Painting, O = Optional, Aftermarket in Gray			

Step	Instruction	Source	Done
		Figure 98	

Step	Instruction	Source	Done
541.	Make 2 of the following assemblies. Paint D81 (2 pcs) and the insides of B82 & B83 with gray primer	M&P	
542.	Paint D81 (2 pcs) with TS-30 Silver Leaf	M&P	
543.	Paint the insides of B82 & B83 with TS-99 IJN Gray	M&P	
544.	Dry fit B83 to B82 as shown in "Figure 98" on page 121	Section 48	
545.	Glue B83 to B82 as shown in "Figure 98" on page 121	Section 48	
546.	Dry fit D81 (2 pcs) to B82/B83 as shown in "Figure 98" on page 121	Section 48	
547.	Glue D81 (2 pcs) to B82/B83 as shown in "Figure 98" on page 121	Section 48	
548.	Dry fit B82 to D84 as shown in "Figure 98" on page 121	Section 48	
549.	Glue B82 to D84 as shown in "Figure 98" on page 121. This Assembly will be referred to as Assembly 48 in future steps.	Section 48	
M&P = Marking and Painting, O = Optional, Aftermarket in Gray			

Step	Instruction	Source	Done

Figure 99

550.	Dry fit Assembly 48 (2 pcs) to the D49 (2 pcs) as shown in "Figure 99" on page 122	Section 49	
551.	Glue Assembly 48 (2 pcs) to the D49 (2 pcs) as shown in "Figure 99" on page 122. Note: we're not going to add the engines to the fuselage just yet. This Assembly will be referred to as Assembly 49 in future steps.	Section 49	

M&P = Marking and Painting, O = Optional, Aftermarket in Gray

Step	Instruction	Source	D o n e
		Figure 100	
552.	Dry fit D85 to Assembly 49 as shown in "Figure 100" on page 123 **(skip if you have Barracuda)**	Section 49	
553.	Glue Dry fit D85 to Assembly 49 as shown in "Figure 100" on page 123 **(skip if you have Barracuda)**. This Assembly will be referred to as Assembly 50 in future steps.	Section 49	
M&P = Marking and Painting, O = Optional, Aftermarket in Gray			

Step	Instruction	Source	D o n e
	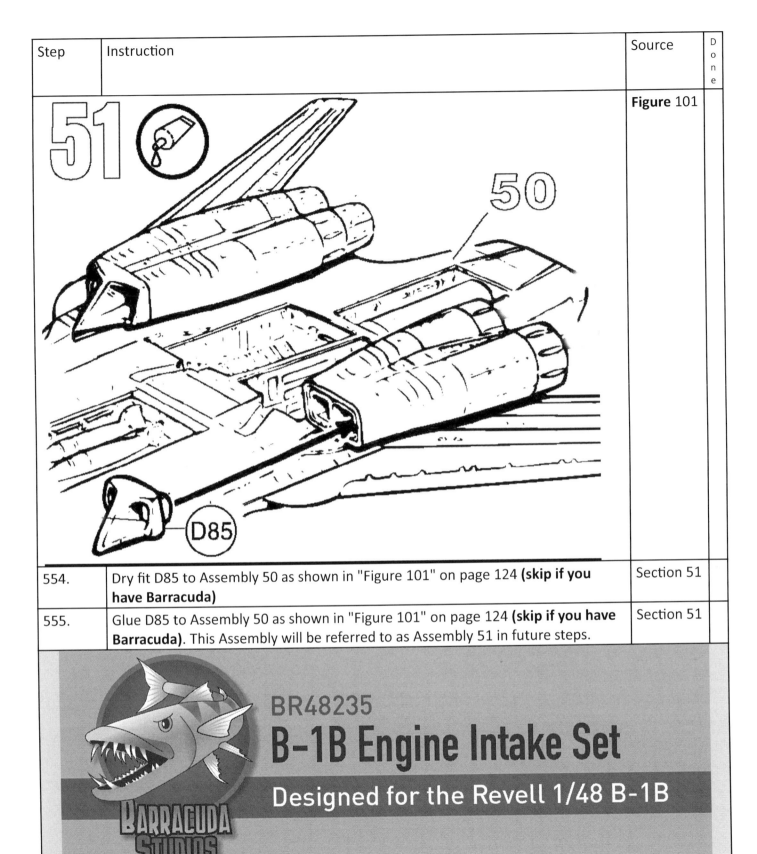	**Figure** 101	
554.	Dry fit D85 to Assembly 50 as shown in "Figure 101" on page 124 **(skip if you have Barracuda)**	Section 51	
555.	Glue D85 to Assembly 50 as shown in "Figure 101" on page 124 **(skip if you have Barracuda)**. This Assembly will be referred to as Assembly 51 in future steps.	Section 51	

M&P = Marking and Painting, O = Optional, Aftermarket in Gray

Step	Instruction	Source	Done
	Remove guard	**Figure** 102	
556.	This set contains 2 engine pod intake castings and 4 separate intake covers. The intakes are much more accurately shaped and represent the auxiliary intake lips in the open position. Some hand work with epoxy putty or filler of your choice will be required to blend these new parts into the kit nacelles. Carefully saw intake castings from mold blocks. Cleanup edges. Remove the small block that protects the point at the apex of the intake. Fit the intakes to the nacelles. The cross sections are quite different. The kit nacelle will need to be built up to match the cross section of the new intakes. We suggest using epoxy putty such as Magic sculpt or Milliput.	BR48235	
	BARRACUDACAST BR48237 **B-1B Late Exhausts No Turkey Feathers** Designed for the 1/48th scale Revell B-1B Lancer kit. Fitted on late production B-1Bs.		
	hole	Figure 103	

M&P = Marking and Painting, O = Optional, Aftermarket in Gray

Step	Instruction	Source	Done
557.	Carefully saw mold blocks from the exhaust tube as shown in "Figure 103" on page 125. Clean up rear faces by block sanding to assure that they are flat. Clean up key slots and tabs and test fit the components to make sure they assemble properly.	BR48237	
558.	Dry fit the exhaust tubes in each nacelles (Assembly 51). You'll probably have to cut back on the edge of the kit's nacelles a bit along with shaving down the exhaust tube to get a good fit	BR48237	
559.	Paint each fan blade and inside of each exhaust tube with X-10 Gun Metal	M&P	
560.	Dry fit the fan blade to the rear of each exhaust tube	BR48237	
561.	Glue the fan blade to the rear of each exhaust tube	BR48237	
562.	Dry fit the exhaust tubes in each nacelles again	BR48237	
563.	Glue the exhaust tubes in each nacelles	BR48237	
564.	Cut some of the foam packing that came with the Barracuda kit and jam it in each exhaust tubes to mask it during the next paint steps	M&P	
565.	Paint the left and right engine assemblies with gray primer	M&P	
566.	Paint the left and right engine assemblies with TS-99 IJN Gray	M&P	
567.	Paint the left and right engine assemblies with TS-13 Clear	M&P	

Rockwell B-1B Lancer, 77 Weapons Squadron, USAF Weapons School Dyess AFB, Texas, October 2012

61 (both sides of intake)
48 (both sides of nacelle)
48 (both sides of nacelle)
61 (both sides of intake)

Figure 104

Step	Instruction	Source	Done
568.	Apply decal 61 to both sides of each engine intake (4 pcs) as shown in "Figure 104" on page 126	M&P	
569.	Apply decal 48 to both sides of each engine nacelle (4 pcs) as shown in "Figure 104" on page 126	M&P	
570.	Paint the left and right engine assemblies with TS-80 Flat Clear	M&P	

M&P = Marking and Painting, O = Optional, Aftermarket in Gray

Step	Instruction	Source	Done
	Figure 105	**Figure** 105	
571.	Carefully saw mold blocks from the exhaust nozzle as shown in "Figure 105" on page 127. Clean up rear faces by block sanding to assure that they are flat. Clean up key slots and tabs and test fit the components to make sure they assemble properly.	BR48237	
572.	Test fit the exhaust nozzles to the exhaust tube. Do not assemble the parts yet. This is a good point to paint the interior parts. Google GE F-101 afterburner and study the images for color and finish of the components.	BR48237	
573.	Paint the interior of the exhaust nozzle with TS-10 Gun Metal	M&P	
574.	Rub the interior the exhaust nozzle with Burnt Jet Engine Pigment from AK	M&P, O	
575.	Paint the outside of the exhaust nozzle with TS-42 Light Gun Metal	M&P	
		Figure 105a	

M&P = Marking and Painting, O = Optional, Aftermarket in Gray

Step	Instruction	Source	Done
576.	Assemble exhaust units after painting using CA or 5 minute epoxy. Carefully remove the radius rods from sprue by light repeated cuts with a new hobby blade. Once free, sand or scrape the back face to remove excess resin. Install radius rods into slots at base of exhaust nozzle as shown in "Figure 105a" on page 127. Ball end fits between webs. Secure radius rods with thin CA or thinned white glue.	BR48237	
577.	Paint the outside of Part A again with TS-42 Light Gun Metal	M&P	
578.	Dab on some Exhaust Wash from AK	M&P, O	
		Figure 106	
579.	Dry fit 28 (4 pcs) to D80 (4pcs) as shown in "Figure 106" on page 128 **(skip if you had Barracuda)**	PE 48857	
580.	Glue 28 (4 pcs) to D80 (4pcs) as shown in "Figure 106" on page 128 **(skip if you had Barracuda)**	PE 48857	
		Figure 107	
581.	**Skip all steps in this Figure if you had Barracuda**	O	
582.	Remove the sprue supports from D79 (4 pcs) as shown in "Figure 107" on page 128	Section 47	
583.	Paint D79 (4 pcs) and D80 (4 pcs) with gray primer	M&P	

M&P = Marking and Painting, O = Optional, Aftermarket in Gray

Step	Instruction	Source	Done
584.	Paint D80 (4 pcs) with TS-83 Metallic Silver	M&P	
585.	Paint the insides of D79 (4 pcs) with TS-63 NATO Black	M&P	
586.	Paint the outsides of D79 (4 pcs) withTS-42 Light Gun Metal	M&P	
587.	Dab on some Exhaust Wash from AK	M&P, O	
588.	Dry fit D80 (4 pcs) to D79 (4 pcs) as shown in "Figure 107" on page 128	Section 47	
589.	Glue D80 (4 pcs) to D79 (4 pcs) as shown in "Figure 107" on page 128	Section 47	
		Figure 108	
590.	Dry fit engine exhausts (4 sets) to the engines as shown in "Figure 108" on page 129	Sections 49 and 50	
591.	Glue engine exhausts (4 sets) to the engines as shown in "Figure 108" on page 129	Sections 49 and 50	
M&P = Marking and Painting, O = Optional, Aftermarket in Gray			

Step	Instruction	Source	Done

Figure 109

592.	Dry fit D49 of one engine assembly to the right side of C50 as shown in "Figure 109" on page 130	Section 28	
593.	Glue D49 of one engine assembly to the right side of C50 as shown in "Figure 109" on page 130	Section 28	
594.	Dry fit D49 of one engine assembly to the left side of C50 as shown in "Figure 109" on page 130	Section 28	
595.	Glue D49 of one engine assembly to the left side of C50 as shown in "Figure 109" on page 130	Section 28	

M&P = Marking and Painting, O = Optional, Aftermarket in Gray

Step	Instruction	Source	Done

Figure 110

Step	Instruction	Source
596.	Leave 17 (2 pcs) on the fret for now. Cut 41 (2 pcs) from the fret and dry fit to 17 as shown in "Figure 110" on page 131	PE 48857
597.	Glue 41 to 17 (2 sets) as shown in "Figure 110" on page 131 (still leave it in the fret)	PE 48857
598.	Form 35 as shown in "Figure 110" on page 131	PE 48857
599.	Form 36 as shown in "Figure 110" on page 131	PE 48857
600.	Form 9 (2 pcs) as shown in "Figure 110" on page 131	PE 48857
601.	Paint 17/41 (2 sets), 9 (2 pcs) , 35, and 36 with gray primer	M&P
602.	Paint 17/41 (2 sets), 9 (2 pcs) , and the outsides of 35 and 36 with XF-87 IJN Gray	M&P
603.	Paint the insides of 35 and 36 with X-10 Gun Metal	M&P
604.	I recommend using page 14 of Willy Peeters' book as a reference	O
605.	Remove 17 (2 pcs) from the fret	PE 48857
606.	Dry fit 41 to 9 (2 sets) as shown in "Figure 110" on page 131	PE 48857
607.	Glue 41 to 9 (2 sets) as shown in "Figure 110" on page 131	PE 48857
608.	Dry fit 35 to the center of the right engine as shown in "Figure 110" on page 131	PE 48857
609.	Glue 35 to the center of the right engine as shown in "Figure 110" on page 131. For 35 & 36, I used some thick 2-part epoxy.	PE 48857
610.	Dry fit 9 (1 set) to the center of the right engine as shown in "Figure 110" on page 131	PE 48857
611.	Glue 9 (1 set) to the center of the right engine as shown in "Figure 110" on page 131	PE 48857

M&P = Marking and Painting, O = Optional, Aftermarket in Gray

Step	Instruction	Source	Done
612.	Dry fit 36 to the center of the left engine as shown in "Figure 110" on page 131	PE 48857	
613.	Glue 36 to the center of the left engine as shown in "Figure 110" on page 131	PE 48857	
614.	Dry fit 9 (1 set) to the center of the left engine as shown in "Figure 110" on page 131	PE 48857	
615.	Glue 9 (1 set) to the center of the left engine as shown in "Figure 110" on page 131	PE 48857	
		Figure 111	
616.	**Skip the steps with this Figure if you have the Barracuda Wheel Set**	O	
617.	Make 2 sets. Dry fit 130 to 131 as shown in "Figure 111" on page 132	Section 19	
618.	Glue 130 to 131 as shown in "Figure 111" on page 132	Section 19	
619.	Paint A34A (2 pcs), A34, and A35 with white primer	M&P	
620.	Paint A34A (2 pcs), A34, and A35 with TS-26 Pure White	M&P	
621.	Dry fit A34A in each wheel (no glue) as shown in "Figure 111" on page 132	Sections 20 and 21	
622.	Dry fit A34 in one wheel as shown in "Figure 111" on page 132. This will be referred to as Assembly 20 in future steps	Section 20	
623.	Glue A34 to A34A in Assembly 20 as shown in "Figure 111" on page 132	Section 20	
624.	Dry fit A35 in the other wheel as shown in "Figure 111" on page 132. This will be referred to as Assembly 21 in future steps	Section 21	
625.	Glue A35 to A34A in Assembly 21 as shown in "Figure 111" on page 132	Section 21	
626.	If you have the Barracuda Wheel Set, locate the nose gear wheels and associated masks.	BR48238	
627.	Mask the hubs and paint the wheels with TS-82 Black Rubber.	BR48238	
M&P = Marking and Painting, O = Optional, Aftermarket in Gray			

Step	Instruction	Source	Done
628.	Remove masks from hubs. Mask the wheels and paint the hubs with white primer	BR48238	
629.	Paint the hubs with TS-26 Pure White. Remove masks from wheels	BR48238	

Figure 112

630.	Dry fit A36 to A37 as shown in "Figure 112" on page 133	Section 22	
631.	Glue A36 to A37 as shown in "Figure 112" on page 133	Section 22	
632.	Dry fit A38 to A39 as shown in "Figure 112" on page 133	Section 23	
633.	Glue A38 to A39 as shown in "Figure 112" on page 133	Section 23	
634.	Insert A37 into A38/A39 as shown in "Figure 112" on page 133 (no glue)	Section 23	
635.	Dry fit A42 to A38/A39 as shown in "Figure 112" on page 133	Section 24	
636.	Glue A42 to A38/A39 as shown in "Figure 112" on page 133	Section 24	

M&P = Marking and Painting, O = Optional, Aftermarket in Gray

Step	Instruction	Source	Done
637.	Dry fit A40 to A41 as shown in "Figure 112" on page 133	Section 24	
638.	Glue A40 to A41 as shown in "Figure 112" on page 133	Section 24	
639.	Dry fit A41 to A38/A39 as shown in "Figure 112" on page 133	Section 24	
640.	Glue A41 to A38/A39 as shown in "Figure 112" on page 133	Section 24	

Figure 113

A36, A37

11

2 pcs.

Step	Instruction	Source	Done
641.	Grind down the section of A36/A37 as shown in "Figure 113" on page 134	PE 48857	
642.	Form and dry fit 11 (2 pcs) to A36/A37 as shown in "Figure 113" on page 134	PE 48857	
643.	Glue 11 (2 pcs) to A36/A37 as shown in "Figure 113" on page 134	PE 48857	
644.	This Assembly will be referred to as Assembly 24 in future steps.	Section 24	
645.	Paint Assembly 24 with white primer	M&P	
646.	Paint Assembly 24 with TS-26 Pure White	M&P	
647.	Paint the section of A37 with X-11 Chrome Silver as shown in "Figure 113" on page 134	M&P	

Figure 114

7 (both sides of u/c leg)

12

M&P = Marking and Painting, O = Optional, Aftermarket in Gray

Step	Instruction	Source	Done
648.	Paint the sections of the nose gear with X-22 Clear as shown in "Figure 114" on page 134	M&P	
649.	Apply decal 12 to both sides of the nose gear with X-22 Clear as shown in "Figure 114" on page 134	M&P	
650.	Paint the nose gear with TS-79 Semi-gloss Clear	M&P	
		Figure 115	
651.	Paint A44 (2 pcs) with X-2 White	M&P	
652.	Paint the front of A44 (2 pcs) with X-16 Flat Aluminum as shown in "Figure 115" on page 135	M&P	
653.	Dry fit clear part 43 (2 pcs) to A44 (2 pcs) as shown in "Figure 115" on page 135	Section 25	
654.	Glue clear part 43 (2 pcs) to A44 (2 pcs) as shown in "Figure 115" on page 135	Section 25	
655.	Dry fit A44 (2 pcs) to Assembly 24 as shown in "Figure 115" on page 135	Section 26	
656.	Glue A44 (2 pcs) to Assembly 24 as shown in "Figure 115" on page 135	Section 26	
657.	Dry fit clear part 45 to Assembly 24 as shown in "Figure 115" on page 135	Section 26	
658.	Glue clear part 45 to Assembly 24 as shown in "Figure 115" on page 135. This Assembly will be referred to as Assembly 26 in future steps.	Section 26	
M&P = Marking and Painting, O = Optional, Aftermarket in Gray			

Step	Instruction	Source	Done
		Figure 116	
659.	Dry fit Assembly 20 to Assembly 26 as shown in "Figure 116" on page 136 (no glue)	Section 27	
660.	Dry fit Assembly 21 to Assembly 20 as shown in "Figure 116" on page 136	Section 27	
661.	Glue Assembly 21 to Assembly 20 as shown in "Figure 116" on page 136	Section 27	
662.	If you have the Barracuda Wheel Set, cut off the axle off of Assembly 20 or a short piece of styrene rod and glue it to one of the wheels, insert it thru the nose gear and glue it to the other wheel	BR48238	
663.	This Assembly will be referred to as Assembly 27 in future steps.	Section 27	
M&P = Marking and Painting, O = Optional, Aftermarket in Gray			

Step	Instruction	Source	Done
		Figure 117	
664.	**Skip the steps with this Figure if you have the Barracuda Wheel Set**	O	
665.	Make 8 sets. Dry fit 133 to 132 as shown in "Figure 117" on page 137	Section 52	
666.	Glue 133 to 132 as shown in "Figure 117" on page 137	Section 52	
667.	Paint A88 (8 pcs), A89 (4 pcs), and A90 (4 pcs) with white primer	M&P	
668.	Paint A88 (8 pcs), A89 (4 pcs), and A90 (4 pcs) with TS-26 Pure White	M&P	
669.	Paint a section of A89 (4 pcs) with X-11 Chrome Silver as shown in "Figure 117" on page 137	M&P	
670.	Dry fit A88 (8 pcs) to a 8 wheels as shown in "Figure 117" on page 137 (no glue)	Section 53 and 54	
671.	Dry fit A89 (4 pcs) to A88 in 4 wheels as shown in "Figure 117" on page 137	Section 53	
672.	Glue A89 (4 pcs) to A88 in 4 wheels as shown in "Figure 117" on page 137. This will be referred to as Assembly 53 in future steps	Section 53	
673.	Dry fit A90 (4 pcs) to A88 in 4 wheels as shown in "Figure 117" on page 137	Section 54	
674.	Glue A90 (4 pcs) to A88 in 4 wheels as shown in "Figure 117" on page 137. This will be referred to as Assembly 54 in future steps	Section 54	
675.	If you have the Barracuda Wheel Set, locate the main landing gear wheels and associated masks.	BR48238	
676.	Mask the hubs and paint the wheels with TS-82 Black Rubber.	BR48238	
677.	Remove masks from hubs. Mask the wheels and paint the hubs with white primer	BR48238	
678.	Paint the hubs with TS-26 Pure White. Remove masks from wheels	BR48238	
M&P = Marking and Painting, O = Optional, Aftermarket in Gray			

Step	Instruction	Source	Done

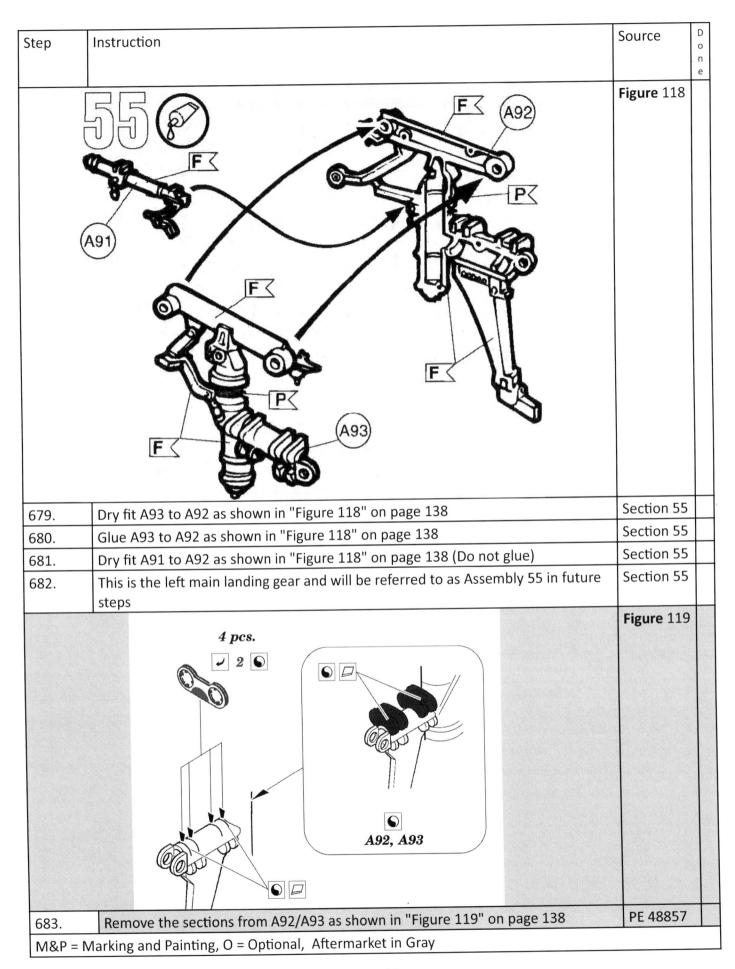

Figure 118

679.	Dry fit A93 to A92 as shown in "Figure 118" on page 138	Section 55	
680.	Glue A93 to A92 as shown in "Figure 118" on page 138	Section 55	
681.	Dry fit A91 to A92 as shown in "Figure 118" on page 138 (Do not glue)	Section 55	
682.	This is the left main landing gear and will be referred to as Assembly 55 in future steps	Section 55	

Figure 119

4 pcs.

A92, A93

| 683. | Remove the sections from A92/A93 as shown in "Figure 119" on page 138 | PE 48857 | |

M&P = Marking and Painting, O = Optional, Aftermarket in Gray

Step	Instruction	Source	Done
684.	Cut slots in A92/A93 as shown in "Figure 119" on page 138	PE 48857	
685.	Form and dry fit 2 (4pcs) to A92/A93 as shown in "Figure 119" on page 138	PE 48857	
686.	Glue 2 (4pcs) to A92/A93 as shown in "Figure 119" on page 138	PE 48857	
		Figure 120	
687.	Dry fit A94 to Assembly 55 as shown in "Figure 120" on page 139	Section 56	
688.	Glue A94 to Assembly 55 as shown in "Figure 120" on page 139. This will be referred to as Assembly 56 in future steps.	Section 56	
		Figure 121	
689.	Dry fit A95 to A96 as shown in "Figure 121" on page 139. I found A96 was a little short when dry fitting it to the wheel well. Using a styrene rod of the same diameter and a glued 1/4 piece to A96	Section 57	
690.	Glue A95 to A96 as shown in "Figure 121" on page 139. This will be referred to as Assembly 57 in future steps.	Section 57	
M&P = Marking and Painting, O = Optional, Aftermarket in Gray			

Step	Instruction	Source	Done
		Figure 122	
691.	Dry fit A97 to Assembly 56 as shown in "Figure 122" on page 140	Section 58	
692.	Glue A97 to Assembly 56 as shown in "Figure 122" on page 140. This will be referred to as Assembly 58 in future steps.	Section 58	
		Figure 123	
693.	Dry fit Assembly 57 to Assembly 58 as shown in "Figure 123" on page 140	Section 59	
694.	Glue Assembly 57 to Assembly 58 as shown in "Figure 123" on page 140. This will be referred to as Assembly 59 in future steps.	Section 59	
M&P = Marking and Painting, O = Optional, Aftermarket in Gray			

Step	Instruction	Source	Done
		Figure 124	
695.	Paint Assembly 59, A98, and A97 with white primer	M&P	
696.	Paint Assembly 59, A98, and A97 with TS-26 Pure White	M&P	
697.	Paint sections of Assembly 59 with X-11 Chrome Silver as shown in "Figure 118" on page 138 and as shown in "Figure 120" on page 139	M&P	
698.	**Caution: adding the main landing gear to the wheel well can be frustrating and test your patience. I highly recommend that you dry fit Assembly 59 to the wheel well without the tires first as shown in "Figure 136" on page 151**	O	
699.	Dry fit 2 Assembly 53's thru A98 thru Assembly 59 thru A99 and to 2 Assembly 54's as shown in "Figure 124" on page 141	Section 60	
700.	Glue 2 Assembly 53's to 2 Assembly 54's as shown in "Figure 124" on page 141. This is the right main landing gear and will be referred to as Assembly 60 in future steps	Section 60	
701.	If you have the Barracuda Wheel Set, cut off the axle off of Assembly 53 and insert it into Assembly 59. Dry fit and glue A98 and A99. Unfortunately, the axle opening in this wheel set is too large. You can't use a larger diameter styrene rod because it would not fit thru A98 and A99 and if you try to enlarge A98 and A99, there's a high risk of damaging them. I also recommend adding the Barracuda tires after the gear has been glued to the wheel well so you can make sure they line up straight and level. I used some generous globs of 2-part epoxy and clamped the Barracuda wheel to the short piece of axle and A98 or A99.	BR48238	
M&P = Marking and Painting, O = Optional, Aftermarket in Gray			

Step	Instruction	Source	Done
		Figure 125	

702.	Dry fit A101 to A100 as shown in "Figure 125" on page 142	Section 61	
703.	Glue A101 to A100 as shown in "Figure 125" on page 142	Section 61	
704.	Dry fit A91 to A100 as shown in "Figure 125" on page 142 (Do not glue)	Section 61	
705.	This is the right main landing gear and will be referred to as Assembly 61 in future steps	Section 61	
		Figure 126	

4 pcs.

A100, A101

| 706. | Remove the sections of A100/A101 as shown in "Figure 126" on page 142 | PE 48857 | |

M&P = Marking and Painting, O = Optional, Aftermarket in Gray

Step	Instruction	Source	Done
707.	Cut slots in A100/A101 as shown in "Figure 126" on page 142	PE 48857	
708.	Form and dry fit 2 (4 pcs) to A100/A101 as shown in "Figure 126" on page 142	PE 48857	
709.	Glue 2 (4 pcs) to A100/A101 as shown in "Figure 126" on page 142	PE 48857	
		Figure 127	
710.	Dry fit A101 to Assembly 61 as shown in "Figure 127" on page 143	Section 62	
711.	Glue A101 to Assembly 61 as shown in "Figure 127" on page 143. This will be referred to as Assembly 62 in future steps.	Section 62	
		Figure 128	
712.	Dry fit A103 to A104 as shown in "Figure 128" on page 143. I found A104 was a little short when dry fitting it to the wheel well. Using a styrene rod of the same diameter and a glued 1/4 piece to A104	Section 63	
713.	Glue A103 to A104 as shown in "Figure 128" on page 143. This will be referred to as Assembly 63 in future steps.	Section 63	
M&P = Marking and Painting, O = Optional, Aftermarket in Gray			

Step	Instruction	Source	Done
	Figure 129	**Figure** 129	
714.	Dry fit A97 to Assembly 62 as shown in "Figure 129" on page 144	Section 64	
715.	Glue A97 to Assembly 62 as shown in "Figure 129" on page 144. This will be referred to as Assembly 64 in future steps.	Section 64	
		Figure 130	
716.	Dry fit Assembly 63 to Assembly 64 as shown in "Figure 130" on page 144	Section 65	
717.	Glue Assembly 63 to Assembly 64 as shown in "Figure 130" on page 144. This will be referred to as Assembly 65 in future steps.	Section 65	
M&P = Marking and Painting, O = Optional, Aftermarket in Gray			

Step	Instruction	Source	Done
		Figure 131	
718.	Paint Assembly 65, A98, and A99 with white primer	M&P	
719.	Paint Assembly 65, A98, and A99 with TS-26 Pure White	M&P	
720.	Paint sections of Assembly 65 with X-11 Chrome Silver as shown in "Figure 125" on page 142 and as shown in "Figure 127" on page 143	M&P	
721.	**Caution: adding the main landing gear to the wheel well can be frustrating and test your patience. I highly recommend that you dry fit Assembly 65 to the wheel well without the tires first as shown in "Figure 135" on page 149**	O	
722.	Dry fit 2 Assembly 53's thru A99 thru Assembly 65 thru A98 to 2 Assembly 54's as shown in "Figure 131" on page 145	Section 66	
723.	Glue 2 Assembly 53's to 2 Assembly 54's as shown in "Figure 131" on page 145. This is the left main landing gear and will be referred to as Assembly 66 in future steps	Section 66	
724.	If you have the Barracuda Wheel Set, cut off the axle off of Assembly 53 and insert it into Assembly 65. Dry fit and glue A98 and A99. Unfortunately, the axle opening in this wheel set is too large. You can't use a larger diameter styrene rod because it would not fit thru A98 and A99 and if you try to enlarge A98 and A99, there's a high risk of damaging them. I also recommend adding the Barracuda tires after the gear has been glued to the wheel well so you can make sure they line up straight and level. I used some generous globs of 2-part epoxy and clamped the Barracuda wheel to the short piece of axle and A98 or A99.	BR48238	
M&P = Marking and Painting, O = Optional, Aftermarket in Gray			

Step	Instruction	Source	Done
		Figure 132	
725.	Remove any masking and move A9 out of the way. Dry fit Assembly 27 to the nose gear wheel well and position A9 as shown in "Figure 132" on page 146	Section 73	
726.	Glue Assembly 27 to the nose gear wheel well and A9 as shown in "Figure 132" on page 146	Section 73	
727.	Dry fit B46 to the nose gear wheel well as shown in "Figure 132" on page 146	Section 73	
728.	Glue B46 to the nose gear wheel well as shown in "Figure 132" on page 146	Section 73	
729.	Dry fit B47 to the nose gear wheel well as shown in "Figure 132" on page 146	Section 73	
730.	Glue B47 to the nose gear wheel well as shown in "Figure 132" on page 146	Section 73	
731.	Dry fit B48 to the nose gear wheel well as shown in "Figure 132" on page 146	Section 73	
732.	Glue B48 to the nose gear wheel well as shown in "Figure 132" on page 146	Section 73	
M&P = Marking and Painting, O = Optional, Aftermarket in Gray			

Step	Instruction	Source	Done
	Figure 133		
733.	Form and dry fit 12 on each side of the nose gear wheel well as shown in "Figure 133" on page 147	PE 48857	
734.	Glue 12 on each side of the nose gear wheel well as shown in "Figure 133" on page 147	PE 48857	
735.	Paint each 12 with X-2 White	M&P	
	Figure 134		
736.	Paint A120 (2 pcs) with white primer	M&P	
737.	Paint A120 (2 pcs) with TS-26 Pure White (according to Willy Peeter's book)	M&P	
738.	Open the ladder door and extend the ladder (Assembly 1)	Section 74	
739.	Dry fit A120 to inside the ladder well on the left and the ladder as shown in "Figure 134" on page 147	Section 74	
740.	Glue A120 to inside the ladder well on the left and the ladder as shown in "Figure 134" on page 147	Section 74	
M&P = Marking and Painting, O = Optional, Aftermarket in Gray			

Step	Instruction	Source	Done
741.	Dry fit A120 to inside the ladder well on the right (not shown)	Section 74	
742.	Glue A120 to inside the ladder well on the right (not shown)	Section 74	
M&P = Marking and Painting, O = Optional, Aftermarket in Gray			

Step	Instruction		Source	Done

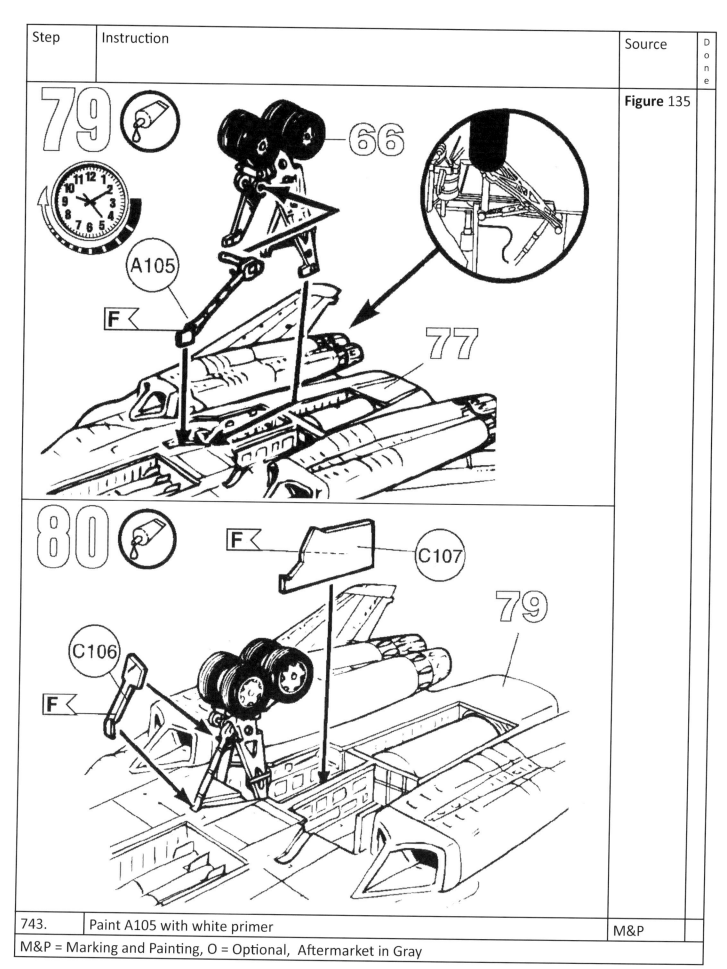

79 — 66 — 77 — A105 — F

80 — C107 — F — C106 — F — 79

Figure 135

743.	Paint A105 with white primer	M&P	

M&P = Marking and Painting, O = Optional, Aftermarket in Gray

Step	Instruction	Source	Done
744.	Paint A105 with TS-26 Pure White	M&P	
745.	Open C106 and C107 that were closed previously for painting	M&P	
746.	Dry fit Assembly 66 to the Assembly 77 as shown in "Figure 135" on page 149	Section 79	
747.	Glue Assembly 66 to the Assembly 77 as shown in "Figure 135" on page 149	Section 79	
748.	Dry fit A105 to Assembly 66 and Assembly 77 as shown in "Figure 135" on page 149	Section 79	
749.	Glue A105 to Assembly 66 and Assembly 77 as shown in "Figure 135" on page 149	Section 79	
750.	Dry fit C106 to A105 as shown in "Figure 135" on page 149	Section 80	
751.	Glue C106 to A105 as shown in "Figure 135" on page 149	Section 80	
752.	Glue C107 to the wheel well as shown in "Figure 135" on page 149	Section 80	
M&P = Marking and Painting, O = Optional, Aftermarket in Gray			

Step	Instruction	Source	Done

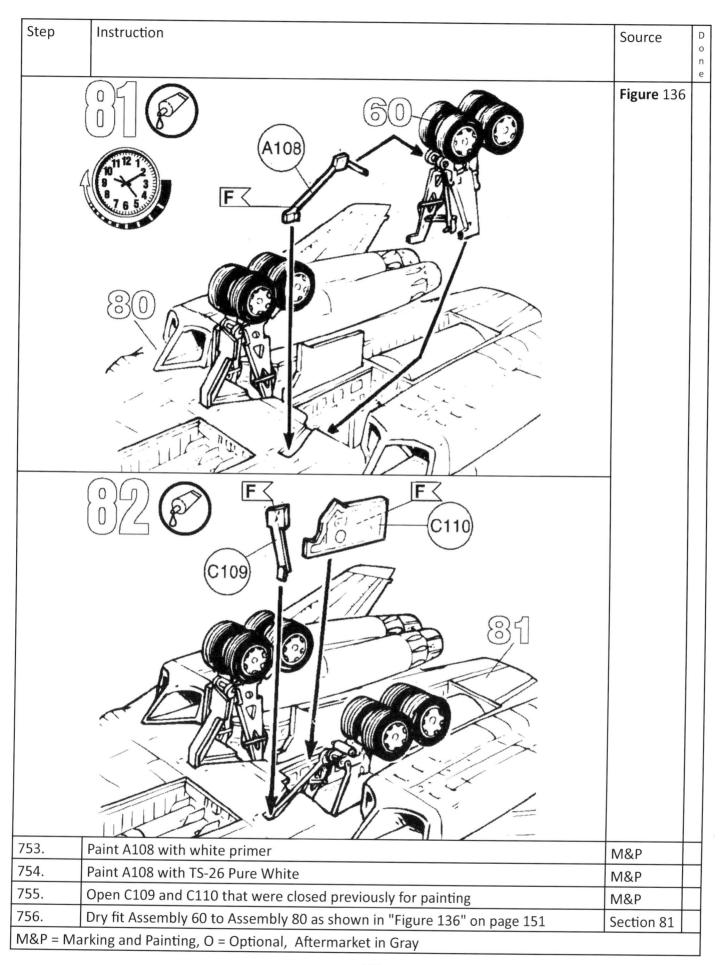

753.	Paint A108 with white primer	M&P	
754.	Paint A108 with TS-26 Pure White	M&P	
755.	Open C109 and C110 that were closed previously for painting	M&P	
756.	Dry fit Assembly 60 to Assembly 80 as shown in "Figure 136" on page 151	Section 81	
M&P = Marking and Painting, O = Optional, Aftermarket in Gray			

Step	Instruction	Source	D o n e
757.	Glue Assembly 60 to Assembly 80 as shown in "Figure 136" on page 151	Section 81	
758.	Dry fit A108 to Assembly 60 and Assembly 80 as shown in "Figure 136" on page 151	Section 81	
759.	Glue A108 to Assembly 60 and Assembly 80 as shown in "Figure 136" on page 151	Section 81	
760.	Dry fit C109 to A108 as shown in "Figure 136" on page 151	Section 82	
761.	Glue C109 to A108 as shown in "Figure 136" on page 151	Section 82	
762.	Glue C110 to the wheel well as shown in "Figure 136" on page 151	Section 82	
		Figure 137	
763.	Open C86 and C87 that were closed for painting earlier	Section 78	
764.	Glue C86 to the wheel well as shown in "Figure 137" on page 152	Section 78	
765.	Glue C87 to the wheel well as shown in "Figure 137" on page 152	Section 78	
		Figure 138	
766.	Open the 6 weapon bay doors the were closed previously for painting	M&P	

M&P = Marking and Painting, O = Optional, Aftermarket in Gray

Step	Instruction	Source	Done
767.	For each door, dry fit 4 C111's as shown in "Figure 138" on page 152	Section 83	
768.	Glue 4 C111's to each of the 6 doors as shown in "Figure 138" on page 152. These will be referred to as Assembly 83 in future steps.	Section 83	
		Figure 139	
769.	Dry fit 2 sets of Assembly 83's to the weapons bays in front of the main landing gear as shown in "Figure 139" on page 153	Section 84	
770.	Glue 2 sets of Assembly 83's to the weapons bays in front of the main landing gear as shown in "Figure 139" on page 153	Section 84	
		Figure 140	
771.	Dry fit 1 set of Assembly 83's to the fuel tank bay aft of the main landing gear as shown in "Figure 140" on page 153	Section 85	
M&P = Marking and Painting, O = Optional, Aftermarket in Gray			

Step	Instruction	Source	Done
772.	Glue 1 set of Assembly 83's to the fuel tank bay aft of the main landing gear as shown in "Figure 140" on page 153	Section 85	
773.	Glue the Sniper Pod assembly to the pylon added in Figure 76	648252	

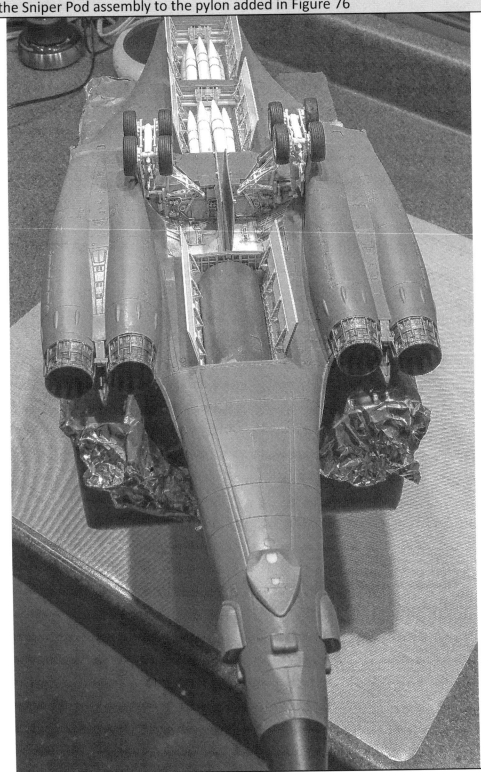

M&P = Marking and Painting, O = Optional, Aftermarket in Gray

Step	Instruction	Source	D o n e

M&P = Marking and Painting, O = Optional, Aftermarket in Gray

Step	Instruction	Source	D o n e
	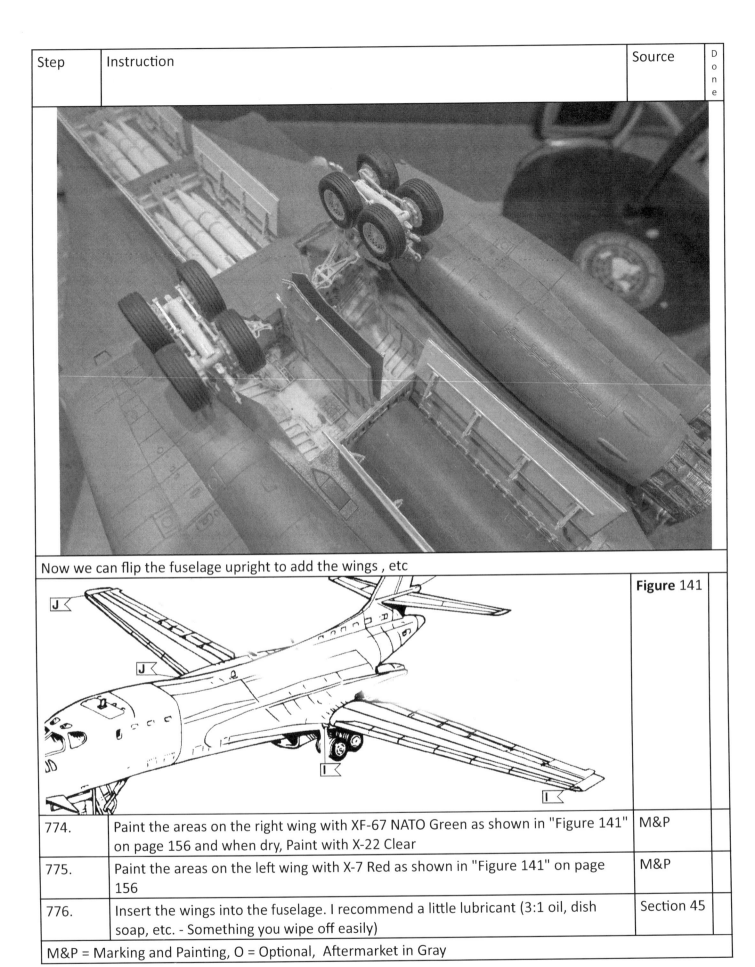 Now we can flip the fuselage upright to add the wings , etc		
		Figure 141	
774.	Paint the areas on the right wing with XF-67 NATO Green as shown in "Figure 141" on page 156 and when dry, Paint with X-22 Clear	M&P	
775.	Paint the areas on the left wing with X-7 Red as shown in "Figure 141" on page 156	M&P	
776.	Insert the wings into the fuselage. I recommend a little lubricant (3:1 oil, dish soap, etc. - Something you wipe off easily)	Section 45	
M&P = Marking and Painting, O = Optional, Aftermarket in Gray			

Step	Instruction	Source	Done
777.	If you want to display the wings extended, install B127 & B128 as shown in "Figure 91" on page 111	Section 88	
	Mike Valdez photo	Figure 142	
778.	If you have the Barracuda B-1B Engine Intake Set Remove the intake covers by sawing off the block then removing the rib with nippers. Test fit and sand as needed. Make sure there is a little play to allow for the thickness of paint on the intake and intake covers. Intake covers are usually painted red. Some covers have the aircraft's number painted on them. Others may have squadron badges.	BR48235	
M&P = Marking and Painting, O = Optional, Aftermarket in Gray			

Final Photos

This model was too big for my photo studio so I had to take the pictures in my kitchen

Coat the wing connection areas with some oil (on the wing and the fuselage post, jockey them around a bit and slip them in place.

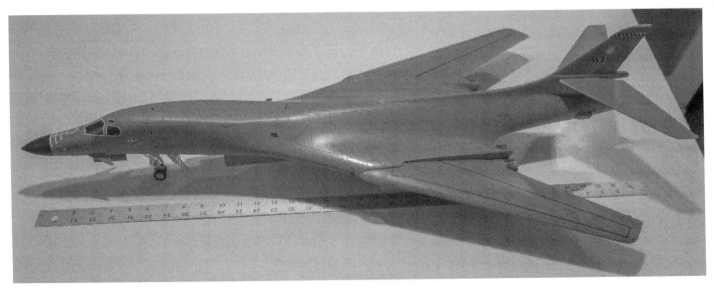

This model is about 36 inches long

And with the wings spread, its about 35 inches across

With the wings swept back is measures about 19.75 inches across

159

161

Here it rests in my large display case

Sprue Index

D